STUDY

REW
URES
n in
ible
FOR
Progressive
Christians

**DONALD
SCHMIDT**

**A SEVEN SESSION
STUDY GUIDE**

BIBLE STUDY

Women in the Bible

HEBREW SCRIPTURES

FOR Progressive Christians

WOOD LAKE

Editor: Michael Schwartzentruber
Proofreader: Dianne Greenslade
Designer: Robert MacDonald

Library and Archives Canada Cataloguing in Publication
Title: Women in the Bible for progressive Christians : Hebrew scriptures : a seven session study guide / Donald Schmidt.
Names: Schmidt, Donald, 1959- author.
Description: Series statement: Bible study | Includes bibliographical references.
Identifiers: Canadiana (print) 20210189398 | Canadiana (ebook) 20210189428 | ISBN 9781773434186 (softcover) | ISBN 9781773434193 (HTML)
Subjects: LCSH: Women in the Bible. | LCSH: Bible. Old Testament – Criticism, interpretation, etc.
Classification: LCC BS575 .S36 2021 | DDC 220.8/3054–dc23

Copyright © 2021 Donald Schmidt
All rights reserved. No part of this publication may be reproduced – except in the case of brief quotations embodied in critical articles and reviews – stored in an electronic retrieval system, or transmitted in any form or by any means, electronic, mechanical, photocopying, recording, or otherwise, without prior written permission of the publisher or copyright holder.

All scripture quotations are from the *Common English Bible* copyright 2011, Abingdon, Nashville, TN. Used by permission.

ISBN 978-1-77343-418-6

Published by Wood Lake Publishing Inc.
485 Beaver Lake Road, Kelowna, BC Canada V4V 1S5
www.woodlake.com | 250.766.2778

Wood Lake Publishing acknowledges the financial support of the Government of Canada.
Wood Lake also acknowledges the financial support of the Province of British Columbia through the Book Publishing Tax Credit.

Wood Lake Publishing acknowledges that we operate in the unceded territory of the Syilx/Okanagan People, and we work to support reconciliation and challenge the legacies of colonialism. The Syilx/Okanagan territory is a diverse and beautiful landscape of deserts and lakes, alpine forests and endangered grasslands. We honour the ancestral stewardship of the Syilx/Okanagan People.

Printed in Canada. Printing 10 9 8 7 6 5 4 3 2 1

CONTENTS

Acknowledgements and Dedication 6

How to Use This Book 7

Preface 10

Session 1: Biblical Women:

    Eve 11

Session 2: Women Caught in Men's Power Struggles:

    Bathsheba and Vashti 25

Session 3: Women Who Are Survivors:

    Tamar and Esther 35

Session 4: Women Who Are Outsiders:

    Rahab and Ruth 48

Session 5: Two Mothers:

    Hagar and Sarah 65

Session 6: Women of the Exodus:

    Puah, Shiphrah, and Miriam 81

Session 7: Two Fiery Women:

    Deborah and Jael 91

Endnotes 101

Bibliography 102

Acknowledgements

Huge thanks go to all those who helped shape this book and who helped me – a simple man – to gain insights on writing a study on stories about women. Specifically, a shoutout goes to those who read the manuscript and participated in conversation and feedback: Gillian Hogan, Ivy Thomas, Judy Valks, Maren Tirabassi, Marty Connor, Meg Jordan, Myrna Stark Leader, Nancy Hillmer, Susan Burt, and 'Anela Rosa.

Thanks as always to everyone at Wood Lake Publishing – Deb MacDonald, Patty Berube, Mike Schwartzentruber, and Robert MacDonald – who believe in offering the world and the church alternative ways of looking at things.

Dedication

I dedicate this book to my dear friend and former colleague Susan Burt, who has so often pushed me to see things differently, to appreciate stories from other perspectives, and to challenge assumptions at every step. I also dedicate it to all the women who, in large and small ways, helped me grow in my faith and as a person.

HOW TO USE THIS BOOK

BIBLE STUDY

HEBREW SCRIPTURES
Women in the Bible
FOR Progressive Christians

For group study

This book is designed to be used in group settings, with minimal preparation by leaders. It is intended to encourage open conversation, for which this study guide is simply that – a guide. Here are some suggested ways you might lead this study, but please, make it work for you!

Begin by inviting any questions or thoughts people have had since the last session. Sometimes a person has had a thought or question lurking in their mind, and it is good to give them a chance to share it.

Assuming participants have read the session material in advance of gathering, invite any additional questions or issues people hope might be addressed. If meeting in person, post a large sheet of paper on the wall and invite people to jot down their questions when they come in. This can provide a sense of anonymity and gives a chance for everyone to look at them as a group and to consider them in a manner that makes sense. At the end of the session, allow time to look once again at the list of questions and make sure they have been covered.

If meeting virtually (such as via Zoom), someone can simply keep the question list and raise them. People can also send questions through "chat" as they join the session.

Begin with the questions at the end of each chapter. Conversation will sometimes move you back into the text to explore something in particular; sometimes it will draw in one or more of the questions on the sheet; and sometimes it will lead to other questions – all of which is a great part of the mix!

As facilitator, your key job is to keep the conversation on track, and to mediate should there happen to be an entanglement. (This rarely happens.)

Perhaps the most important guideline is the need for mutual respect. Even if there are disagreements, we need to respect the opinions and thoughts of others in the group. All opinions are valid,

BIBLE STUDY

HEBREW SCRIPTURES
Women in the Bible
FOR Progressive Christians

even ones we may not agree with. The process of learning will from time-to-time result in some disagreement, which is okay when handled with respect.

Similarly, it is good to remind participants that emotions can run high or we may feel more exposed when we are dealing with issues of faith, which suggests we should tread gently with one another, especially when we sense that an issue might be particularly close for someone in the group.

It is important to remember that none of us are more "right" than the others in the group. This book does not pretend to provide an authoritative voice on anything; rather, in these pages I have sought to bring out a variety of thoughts and opinions that I have encountered over the years, and to put them forward to provoke thought and conversation. Just because I have written something down does not mean you are not free to disagree with the book – and with the facilitator – as well as with each other. The key is to do it with respect for one another.

For individual study

The best thing to do is read the study guide, with a Bible close at hand. While the biblical stories are included in the guide you may want to explore what came before or comes after.

Mark the study guide with interesting things you learn from other sources, or with questions. Spend time pondering the questions. You might wish to write responses in the margins, but it's far more important simply to let the questions guide your thinking and reflection.

A note on dates and translations

Throughout this book we use the common designations "BCE" (Before the Common Era) and "CE" (Common Era) rather than the archaic BC and AD, because BCE and CE are more inclusive of all people! The numbers involved in the dates do not change.

There are many good biblical translations of the Bible and in general I encourage you to use the one you like best. A few comments about some translations:

- *The King James Version* It is lovely English poetry, but not a very good translation. The manuscripts used for the translation have in recent centuries been supplanted by hundreds of other older and far more accurate ones. Additionally, because none of us speak 17th-century English it can take more time translating the King James English into modern English than anything else. It is not helpful for study.

- *New Revised Standard Version* Done by a group of scholars in the latter part of the 20th century, this translation has generally been held up as being incredibly accurate due to the diligence of a vast editorial team. On the downside, in order to keep it textually close to the original, readability is often lost and the text can feel a bit stiff and stilted to some ears. It was also translated at a fairly high reading level.

- *Common English Bible* is the translation used in this study guide. That does not make it the "best," but I find it accurate, up-to-date, and highly readable.

- *The Voice* This version can be especially helpful for those who may not have a lot of biblical background and who struggle sometimes to understand what certain biblical passages mean. The translators (slightly conservative) have occasionally added text. Whenever they do so, the additional text appears in *italics* so you can tell at a glance where the additions are. These additions help flesh out the text and can provide helpful context, especially given that we are dealing with stories that are thousands of years old and took place in a culture and religious milieu very different from our own.

- *The Message* This paraphrase by Eugene Peterson, with the assistance of several other modern scholars, is arguably one of the most popular versions of the Bible in English. Peterson worked from the original-language texts (Hebrew and Greek). At times, Peterson uses more words than other versions in order to convey not just the literal sense of the biblical message, but the emotional sense. It is amongst the most readable of all Bible versions.

BIBLE STUDY

HEBREW SCRIPTURES
Women in the Bible
FOR Progressive Christians

BIBLE STUDY

HEBREW
SCRIPTURES
Women in the Bible
FOR
Progressive
Christians

Preface

Many years ago, when I moved to Hawaii to serve a church there, I asked a friend to give me some guidelines. Hawaiian culture is very different from my own (I'm a Caucasian Canadian) and I wanted to make sure I could connect with the people in the congregation. My friend, who had lived all his life in Hawaii, gave me some very sound advice.

"Listen very carefully to what they don't say between the sentences." At first, I didn't understand, but over time his words came to make a lot of sense.

"Listen very carefully to what they don't say between the sentences." That is what we must do when we approach stories about women in the Bible.

As we read these ancient texts, written almost exclusively by men in a male-dominated society, it can at times seem astonishing that there is any acknowledgement of women at all. In the book *Scripture Windows*, author Peter Pitzele speaks of how the Torah is written, "'black fire on white fire.' The black fire refers to the words, the writings; the white fire refers to the space, the gaps between the words, what is not written. Some say that what the writer does not say matters more than what is written."[1]

When you add to this the ways in which we have used and abused the Bible for thousands of years, one could almost be forgiven for assuming that there were no women in that world at all. Reading the Bible is almost like reading Margaret Atwood's *The Handmaid's Tale,* in which women were reduced to baby-making entities and little else.

Consequently, when we encounter a snippet of a woman's story, we need to pause and attempt to read what else is there – at times to reconstruct, at others to fill in the blanks, and in general to assume there is always more to the story than meets the eye. Regardless of our own gender and sexuality, we must remember that we can learn much about the world by reading these stories. These ancient women, rather than being confined to history, are very much alive within the ongoing story of our faith. We must let their stories enter our being and become a part of our lives.

SESSION 1

Biblical Women: Eve

Before we tackle the story of Eve found in Genesis, it is important to step back and take a much broader look at women in the Bible.

Women make up over half of the world's population and yet throughout vast portions of history, in far too many cultures and traditions, women have been kept out of power; they have been oppressed and disregarded and have often had their stories ignored. This is a tragedy not only for women, but for all of humankind. We all have much to gain by hearing one another's stories and by experiencing other people in all their rich fullness – not from a preconceived notion that one group or sex is superior to another.

Implicit in this view is the understanding that we are all different. Men and women are different from each other and within each gender there are many differences and variants. We – all of us – live on a wide spectrum of identity, which is precisely *why* we need to hear each other's stories.

This is one of the greatest gifts our Creator has given us: the wonderful and amazing gift of difference. We are, as South African Archbishop Desmond Tutu once said, the "rainbow people of God." Except in the human rainbow there are more colours than we could ever imagine.

All of this is important to note at the outset, because the bulk of our history has been told by men. Whether they did a good job or not isn't really the point; what *is* important is that the stories we have preserved from ancient times tell things from a cultural perspective that was androcentric, from within a patriarchal society, and they often ignore women. Thus, we need to look between the lines and behind the words to find the stories of truly significant women in our scriptures and, by extension, our tradition.

A classic case in point, the vast majority of genealogies do not include any women. Does that mean that somehow the men had children all on their own? I'm guessing not – and I say that with

BIBLE STUDY

HEBREW SCRIPTURES
Women in the Bible
FOR Progressive Christians

my tongue planted firmly in cheek. When we look at a biblical genealogy, then, we should not gloss over the fact that women are not present, but instead ask who they might be, and what their stories might be.

By the same token, whenever we read scripture and encounter a woman – either named directly, or implied – we need to pause and attempt to reconstruct her story, however we can. In so doing, we experience scripture from another angle. This is not to fault the (almost exclusively male) writers who told the stories, but simply to give fuller recognition to those whose stories were not included, or were included without much mention. Throughout the sessions that make up this study I invite you to explore these women's stories, and to learn from them.

Some people wonder if we dare impose our values from the 21st century onto ancient texts. I think we must do so cautiously, but directly. We need not judge the ancient stories for what they told, or the storytellers for how they told them, but we can question them, and we can wonder about them, and we can look for the pieces that may have been left out. From my perspective, we should never leave someone out of their own story.

The thing is, God has no gender. God is beyond gender. God is greater than gender. But our language – the beloved English of Shakespeare and of King James – is fiercely limited. It was only in the final decades of the 20th century that we dared to move away from the practice of using the masculine "men" and "man" as supposedly "inclusive" terms. Many people simply couldn't hear the masculine terms as inclusive – quite the opposite in fact. Despite this change, we are so used to hearing male terminology, and to understanding males as primary, and so many people want to continue to using exclusively male pronouns for God, it is possible we will struggle with how to express ourselves for generations to come.

So let us be clear: the problem is with our language, not with God. The sexism lies in the way we use language to express ourselves, not in the way God exists. God is not male just because some people prefer to use male pronouns rather than the neutral (and genderless) "it" to refer to the divine. We need to caution ourselves *always* to avoid language that seeks, however inadvertently, to express a sexism that is not present in the original thought.

Consider Genesis 1:27, which I offer here in older and newer versions:

King James Version (1611)
So God created man in his own image, in the image of God created he him; male and female created he them.

Common English Bible (2011)
God created humanity in God's own image, in the divine image God created them, male and female God created them.

One can see at a glance that the *King James Version* uses the male pronouns three times in reference to God, and once in reference to humanity (along with the noun "man"). Yet clearly this is not what was meant, or the passage would make no sense; to say in modern English that God created male and female in "his" image is nonsensical, linguistically and literally.

Translating *ha-adam* as "man" and letting that stand for centuries as an "inclusive" term has caused endless problems, for it has inadvertently allowed our minds to rest with the notion that "male" is the reference point relative to which everything else is defined, and that "female" is somehow secondary. We need to let it sink in that according to Genesis 1 (which does not have the characters "Eve" or "Adam" in it) the humans are equal. They are both created in the image of God and nothing in the text implies that one is more important than the other. If we only had Genesis 1, in theory we would never have had problems with the equality of men and women – at least in the Bible.

All this is to say that we must continue to find new language, and new ways to use our existing cumbersome and at times sexist language, so that we do not perpetuate understandings that were never valid or meant in the first place. Male and female were cre-

BIBLE STUDY

HEBREW
SCRIPTURES
**Women in
the Bible**
FOR
Progressive
Christians

Rewriting history

History is always being rewritten. It is always told by the "victors" and typically reflects primarily or only their perspective on events. Thus, the story they tell casts them in the best possible light.

Haida Gwaii, a set of islands north of Vancouver Island where I was born, provides a good example. Notice the difference in the names: Haida Gwaii is named for the Indigenous people who have lived there for millennia, and Vancouver Island is named for a British explorer who visited there to negotiate a peace treaty among the Indigenous peoples, the Spanish, and the English in 1792.

Haida Gwaii was officially given the name "Queen Charlotte Islands" by British captain George Dixon in 1787. When in 2010 the British Columbia government changed the name back to Haida Gwaii, many people complained that the government was "trying to rewrite history."

The Haida, who first named the land – "Haida Gwaii" literally means "land of the Haida people" – have been present on the islands for between 12,500 and 14,000 years, whereas the islands only bore the name of a queen (who had never visited) for 200 years. So yes, history was being rewritten in 2010. But it had also been rewritten in 1787.

A similar situation arises when we study scripture, and we need to own that up front. Stories and history shift depending on the writer or source. Did Noah take two of each animal onto the ark, or 14? One source, in Genesis 6:19, tells us a pair of each. Genesis 7:2 tells us seven pairs of each. The question is, to what extent does it matter. One writer wanted to emphasize simplicity – one male, one female – because God was starting over again. The other writer wanted to emphasize that this was a holy, God-ordained new beginning and so chose to use the symbolic number seven, which represents perfection. When it comes to ancient stories in the Bible, facts are secondary to meaning and symbolism.

■ What are some examples of "rewriting" history that you have encountered?

■ How do you feel when people remove statues glorifying or commemorating former leaders who caused great harm?

■ How might we tell history more fairly?

ated somehow in God's image – which works if we remember that the Bible does not tell us that God is male, but rather that God transcends humanity and thus gender.

We are left to wonder why some people find it necessary to cling with tightly clenched hands to the notion that God created "man" rather than "human beings" – and that the God who did this must be male. The Bible simply doesn't say those things; these are ideas that were imposed onto the text later, by people who had an agenda that was different than that of the author of Genesis.

Is "history" a sexist word?

Some people believe the word "history" is itself sexist. This idea arises from a basic misunderstanding. Contrary to popular belief, the word is not a construct of "his + story," but rather comes from the Greek word *historia*, which literally, at its most generic level, simply means "inquiry," or the act of seeking knowledge, as well as the knowledge that results from inquiry. In other words, the "his" at the beginning of the Greek word is not a masculine reference of any kind and has no connection to the English word "his." In fact, the Greek word *historia* is a feminine noun. So, while in its current English form the word "history" may appear to be masculine or male-oriented, it is a much older and richer word that should point us in the direction of inquiring deeply and broadly into our past to uncover the stories told by all voices – precisely the goal of this study.

Eve

Eve is the first woman who appears in the Bible. She is only mentioned by name twice in Genesis, and one of those times is simply when she is given her name. She is clearly a made-up character, yet her story is arguably one of the most famous – or infamous, depending on your theological viewpoint – of all time.

It's worth looking at Eve not as an individual woman, but for what her character represents: the quintessential woman from whom all life flows. When we approach her that way and earnestly look at what the Bible says – and especially at what it does *not* say

BIBLE STUDY

HEBREW SCRIPTURES
Women in the Bible
FOR Progressive Christians

BIBLE STUDY

HEBREW
SCRIPTURES
Women in the Bible
FOR
Progressive
Christians

– we gain some fascinating insights into the place of women in the Bible, and how we have distorted their role over the centuries.

The creation story in Genesis 2 and 3 is older than the one in Genesis 1, even though it appears second. Before reading the biblical stories, we should note that neither story is sexist in the way we might understand the term. As mentioned above, the story in Genesis 1 is non-sexist and clearly presents the two beings – male and female – as being equal. Genesis 2:4b–25 tells a different story about the creation of human beings, where one is created before the other. The thing is, we have often assumed that the first being is male (and thus, that the second one would be female), but the Hebrew text does not support that idea. Rather, God creates a genderless "earthling" and sets it to live in the garden. This first earthling is lonely, so God sets out to create a companion for it. There is nothing in the text to suggest that the companion would be anything less than equal to the first being. When all the companions God makes turn out to be unsuitable to the task, God scratches the divine head a little and thinks, "Okay, let's try something else." This is where things get a little complicated – or at least where we have altered the story from its original a little to make it work.

In the traditional understanding, God puts the first earthling (often described as "the man" even though the Hebrew does not say that) to sleep and extracts a rib from which God then creates a second creature and presents it to the first. At this point, gender comes into the story – but still there is nothing to suggest that they are anything other than equals. Unfortunately, the *King James Version* relied on the word "helpmate" to describe the companion. Over time "helpmate" became a loaded word that clearly was meant to imply subservience – "woman" was only a "helper" to the "man," who was primary. Not quite what the text actually says, but tradition ran with it.

A greater complication comes from the Hebrew word *tsela* which is usually translated as "rib." This is a bit curious because most scholars admit that *tsela* is not used that way elsewhere; the word means "side" – not a single bone. Thus, it's more likely the author imagined God separating the ribcage and making two humans from it – two complementary creatures that mirror each other yet have obvious sexual differences. And they are equal.

Even Saint Augustine (hardly the most gender-inclusive of individuals, I'll grant you!) wrote, "If God had meant woman to rule over man he would have taken her out of Adam's head. Had he designed her to be his slave, he would have taken her out of his feet. But God took woman out of man's side, for he made her to be a helpmeet and an equal to him." Leaving aside the sexist language referring to God, and the reference to Adam (who didn't have a name yet in the story), Augustine makes an interesting point: if God created the second human from the side of the first, they are equal. Potent stuff.

The Fall?

Now let's look at the key story about Eve that we find in the Bible – namely the whole man/woman/snake/fruit thing. Some have called it "the fall," but that makes little sense if we recognize that the Bible continues from this point on telling us of God's unending and amazing love for us. If we had in fact fallen, why would God "waste" any time with us? Why wouldn't God just toss us out and try again?

Key behind those questions is the simple reality that, of course, this is a *story*, not a factual account of a historical event. It is an early folktale that was told to try to explain a few things: Why do snakes crawl on their bellies? Why do women experience excruciating pain in childbirth? And why do men have to work so hard all day long, every day, just to get enough food to stave off starvation for another day? Of course, these questions are not the focus of this study. It's more important that we address the elephant in the room – which is to say what Christians have done with this story for centuries, and how we have viewed the woman in the story ever since.

BIBLE STUDY

HEBREW
SCRIPTURES
**Women in
the Bible**
FOR
Progressive
Christians

Genesis 3

The snake was the most intelligent of all the wild animals that the Lord God had made. He said to the woman, "Did God really say that you shouldn't eat from any tree in the garden?"

²The woman said to the snake, "We may eat the fruit of the garden's trees ³but not the fruit of the tree in the middle of the garden. God said, 'Don't eat from it, and don't touch it, or you will die.'"

⁴The snake said to the woman, "You won't die! ⁵God knows that on the day you eat from it, you will see clearly and you will be like God, knowing good and evil." ⁶The woman saw that the tree was beautiful with delicious food and that the tree would provide wisdom, so she took some of its fruit and ate it, and also gave some to her husband, who was with her, and he ate it. ⁷Then they both saw clearly and knew that they were naked. So they sewed fig leaves together and made garments for themselves.

⁸During that day's cool evening breeze, they heard the sound of the Lord God walking in the garden; and the man and his wife hid themselves from the Lord God in the middle of the garden's trees. ⁹The Lord God called to the man and said to him, "Where are you?"

¹⁰The man replied, "I heard your sound in the garden; I was afraid because I was naked, and I hid myself."

¹¹He said, "Who told you that you were naked? Did you eat from the tree, which I commanded you not to eat?"

¹²The man said, "The woman you gave me, she gave me some fruit from the tree, and I ate."

¹³The Lord God said to the woman, "What have you done?!"

And the woman said, "The snake tricked me, and I ate."
¹⁴The Lord God said to the snake,
"Because you did this,
    you are the one cursed
        out of all the farm animals,
        out of all the wild animals.
    On your belly you will crawl,
        and dust you will eat
        every day of your life.
¹⁵I will put contempt
between you and the woman,

between your offspring and hers.
They will strike your head,
    but you will strike at their heels."
¹⁶To the woman he said,
"I will make your pregnancy very painful;
    in pain you will bear children.
You will desire your husband,
    but he will rule over you."
¹⁷To the man he said, "Because you listened to your wife's voice and you ate from the tree that I commanded, 'Don't eat from it,' cursed is the fertile land because of you;
    in pain you will eat from it
    every day of your life.
¹⁸Weeds and thistles will grow for you,
    even as you eat the field's plants;
¹⁹by the sweat of your face you will eat bread –
    until you return to the fertile land,
    since from it you were taken;
    you are soil,
    to the soil you will return."
²⁰The man named his wife Eve because she is the mother of everyone who lives. ²¹The Lord God made the man and his wife leather clothes and dressed them. ²²The Lord God said, "The human being has now become like one of us, knowing good and evil." Now, so he doesn't stretch out his hand and take also from the tree of life and eat and live forever, ²³the Lord God sent him out of the garden of Eden to farm the fertile land from which he was taken. ²⁴He drove out the human. To the east of the garden of Eden, he stationed winged creatures wielding flaming swords to guard the way to the tree of life.

We are told that the snake ("serpent" in older translations) was *arum*. That's the Hebrew word used here and it immediately presents a problem because it is also used in Genesis 2:25 and 3:11, where it is translated as "naked." The majority of English-language translations, however, render *arum* in this passage as something like "shrewd, crafty, cunning" – perhaps seeing in those words something that might be akin to "naked," remembering that naked does not inherently mean *nude* but rather *exposed* or *vulnerable*. No matter how we translate the word at any of these

HEBREW SCRIPTURES
Women in the Bible
FOR Progressive Christians

junctures, the meaning of the word is a bit ambiguous.

The curse to which the woman refers in Genesis 3:3 – "God said, 'Don't eat from it, and don't touch it, or you will die'" – was first uttered back in 2:16–17 where it was said only to the first earthling (the second had not yet been created). Here the woman expands it, adding "don't even touch it."

When the people eat the fruit, they become _____. Fill in the blank with whatever word is used to describe the snake in verse 1, for it is the same word in Hebrew.

We have now arrived at the word "naked" in verse 7 (presumably translated that way because the man and woman sewed fig leaf garments for themselves, and because of the man's response to God in verse 10), but is this specifically because they were naked (as in "nude"), or because they now understood the difference between them and were perhaps confused? We'll never know what the storyteller intended, but the question is worth pondering if for no other reason than it reminds us that this story is not as simple nor as straightforward as we might think.

An odd conversation occurs in 3:9–11, when God asks the couple where they have been and what they have done. One could assume it is a rhetorical device and that God already knows the answer, but why do we think that? Perhaps God – at least in the understanding of this storyteller – does *not* know everything about us. Perhaps that notion developed later.

Continuing on, the man blames the woman, who then blames the snake. Does this really let anyone off the hook? No. This is a vital point. Saying, "I did not kill the person because I did not pull the trigger" does not really count if it turns out you were holding the gun. The man and woman both realize they have done something they shouldn't have done, and neither of them wants to take responsibility for it.

God curses all three of them, beginning with the snake, and ending with the man. The order would not matter except for the fact that tradition has always blamed the woman and has suggested that somehow her punishment was the worst. But there's nothing in the biblical text itself to suggest this; there is only our choice in how we read it and interpret it. In other words, this is a classic case of people believing something and then turning to the Bible to find a way to support their preconceived belief. If we dare to let the story stand on its own, it is simply a tragic tale of three beings doing something wrong, and all three of them being punished – differently but, I would argue, equally.

The curses roughly relate to the ways in which their lives will unfold, which again should not be surprising given that we are dealing with a folktale that was told to try to explain or provide a reason for some of the harsher realities of life. The snake must now crawl on the ground. The woman is told she will have horrific pain in childbirth, and the man is told that he will work every day of his life, just to get enough food to eat.

Verse 16 is problematic if we take the statements as being proscriptive rather than descriptive (big words that roughly mean "as being what God intended versus the situation that we have created"). We are told that the "husband will rule over the wife" – an odd turn of phrase seeing as the two people are not "married." And who exactly, in the context of the story, would oversee the marriage, and why would they marry in the first place given that they are the only two people? Again, these are silly questions the writer simply isn't interested in – that is, assuming this is part of the original text to begin with. Alternatively, the use of "wife" here might be a linguistic clue that this idea was added to the text at a later date.

Traditionally, we have taken this verse to mean that the woman shall be ruled over by the man because she did something wrong. According to the story she did, but so did the man, and so did the snake. Some have suggested that she acted without the man's permission, but let's be clear – absolutely nothing in the text tells us, or frankly even implies, that she needed the man's permission.

"Sin," to use the word most often employed to describe the events of this story, can be understood as the attempt to place ourselves above God, or the presumption to think we know more than God. All of the characters in this story do that, and they all have to live with the consequences. To quote scholar Irvin Busenitz, "Self-exaltation and pride always result in the desire to dominate and rule. Every person to some extent desires to dominate and rule over others ..."[2]

We should also note that the storyteller has the man name the woman "Eve," a word akin to "live" in Hebrew, because she is the mother of all who live. It takes some serious theological twisting – and much of that has been done over the centuries – to assume that the storyteller wants to suggest that the "mother of all who live" is cursed more, or more responsible than the other characters in the story, for what happens. The woman, man, and serpent all sinned – presumably equally.

According to the author, God determines (3:21-24) that the humans now know too much and must be banished from the garden forever. Immediately prior to this, however, God performs a task that we might normally associate with women: God makes clothes for the two humans, lest they venture into the world without cover and protection from the elements. As this story draws to a close, this simple, kindly act shows us a God who cares in the way a parent might care.

Eve appears again very briefly at the start of the next chapter, where we are simply told that she and Adam have sex, and that Eve bears a child named Cain. She then has another son, named Abel.

The story continues, of course, and wanders into territory that doesn't have much relevance in terms of this study, but perhaps it's worth pointing out one more thing. After Cain kills his brother Abel, he goes off to the land of Nod to find a wife. Which begs the question, where did the people of Nod come from? Again, this is the kind of question the storyteller simply wasn't interested in, if the writer thought about it at all. The only reason I mention it at all is because it reminds us that these stories are human inventions, and full of oddities. They are not given to us as "factual history" as we understand the term today, but simply show us how one group of ancient people understood life.

And what did they understand? A few things seem obvious. To them, creation is wonderful, God is good, but something must have happened – specifically, something "we" (humanity) did – to make life so hard. That's really what this story is about. The fact that we have twisted it to suggest that women are responsible for the world's ills and should therefor be punished, or that they are secondary or subordinate creatures to me, is foolish and tragic. The story simply doesn't say that.

Questions

■ How do you understand the creation of human beings in Genesis 1:26? Do you think of it in male-oriented language ("God created man") or more inclusive language ("God created human beings")?

■ Why do you think some people cling to the notion that a male God created "man," as opposed to a genderless God creating humankind? What or who is served by each understanding?

■ How has the use of English, or other modern influences, impacted your understanding of the Bible, specifically regarding the place and role of women?

■ What are ways we can experience the stories of biblical women more fully, given the limited information available, or that we tend to receive?

■ How, if at all, does your understanding of the story in Genesis 2 change if you understand the word generally translated as "rib," as referring to half of the ribcage?

■ Why might translators and interpreters have been keen to perpetuate the idea that woman was created from a single rib?

■ What might happen to our understanding of gender difference if we interpret the story as saying that the two beings, male and female, are equal parts of one whole?

■ Given that the story of the garden is not factual, what can it teach us?

■ Why do you think the storyteller had Eve extend God's original curse by saying "don't even touch that fruit" (or you will die)?

- Nothing in this story suggests that one character – neither the snake, the woman, or the man – is cursed more than another, yet for millennia we have chosen to blame the woman, and to "punish" women in general. Why do you think that is?
- This story ends with the couple being banished from paradise. How do you see this "truth" reflected in the world around us today?
- How does the story change if we see all the figures as disobedient?

SESSION 2

Women Caught in Men's Power Struggles: Bathsheba and Vashti

Far too often we hear stories of women who, supposedly, were in the "wrong place at the wrong time" and who suffered grievously because of it. Yet the truth is, women often suffer these things simply *because* they are women. A woman walks home from work and gets raped on a dark street. Or she is accused of provoking a sexual assault because she chose to wear shorts on a hot day. Men from all walks of life prey on women, who generally have less power than the male aggressor. Afterwards, as we saw in the previous session about Eve, "the story" gets twisted. Suddenly, it's the woman who must have been at fault – the men couldn't help themselves; they were seduced, or it was the woman's fault for making them angry, and on and on it goes.

None of this is new. This type of abuse of women is grounded in our past, in our traditions, and examples of it are certainly present in scripture. This session will look at the stories of two women who were abused. In one story, a woman is raped and gets caught up in a scheme that results in her husband's murder. In the other, a woman is asked to perform a degrading act and refuses.

Bathsheba

2 Samuel 11:1–17, 26–27
In the spring, when kings go off to war, David sent Joab, along with his servants and all the Israelites, and they destroyed the Ammonites, attacking the city of Rabbah. But David remained in Jerusalem.

²One evening, David got up from his couch and was pacing back and forth on the roof of the palace. From the roof he saw a woman bathing; the woman was very beautiful. ³David sent someone and inquired about the woman. The report came back:

BIBLE STUDY

HEBREW SCRIPTURES
Women in the Bible
FOR
Progressive Christians

"Isn't this Eliam's daughter Bathsheba, the wife of Uriah the Hittite?" ⁴So David sent messengers to take her. When she came to him, he had sex with her. (Now she had been purifying herself after her monthly period.) Then she returned home. ⁵The woman conceived and sent word to David.

"I'm pregnant," she said.

⁶Then David sent a message to Joab: "Send me Uriah the Hittite." So Joab sent Uriah to David. ⁷When Uriah came to him, David asked about the welfare of Joab and the army and how the battle was going. ⁸Then David told Uriah, "Go down to your house and wash your feet."

Uriah left the palace, and a gift from the king was sent after him. ⁹However, Uriah slept at the palace entrance with all his master's servants. He didn't go down to his own house. ¹⁰David was told, "Uriah didn't go down to his own house," so David asked Uriah, "Haven't you just returned from a journey? Why didn't you go home?"

¹¹"The chest and Israel and Judah are all living in tents," Uriah told David. "And my master Joab and my master's troops are camping in the open field. How could I go home and eat, drink, and have sex with my wife? I swear on your very life, I will not do that!"

¹²Then David told Uriah, "Stay here one more day. Tomorrow I'll send you back." So Uriah stayed in Jerusalem that day. The next day ¹³David called for him, and he ate and drank, and David got him drunk. In the evening Uriah went out to sleep in the same place, alongside his master's servants, but he did not go down to his own home.

¹⁴The next morning David wrote a letter to Joab and sent it with Uriah. ¹⁵He wrote in the letter, "Place Uriah at the front of the fiercest battle, and then pull back from him so that he will be struck down and die."

¹⁶So as Joab was attacking the city, he put Uriah in the place where he knew there were strong warriors. ¹⁷When the city's soldiers came out and attacked Joab, some of the people from David's army fell. Uriah the Hittite was also killed ...

²⁶When Uriah's wife heard that her husband Uriah was dead, she mourned for her husband. ²⁷After the time of mourning was over, David sent for her and brought her back to his house. She became his wife and bore him a son.

But what David had done was evil in the Lord's eyes.

First and foremost, notice that Bathsheba's story is told as if it were simply a man's story – the significant role she plays (she's only named once in the narrative) is considered secondary. She is an incidental player in the whole thing. Yet how can that be? She is a married woman who is raped and impregnated by another man. That alone would be traumatic enough for any woman but there is more to come.

Before we carry on with the story, though, let's take a step back to see how this first incident is set up. It is the time of year when kings go to war, suggesting this is just something that men (at least leaders) do – they fight. This sets us up for what happens next. David sees a beautiful woman and orders that she be brought to him. There's no debate, there's no back and forth about this – just as men go to war, so they take advantage of women. The two pieces are presented as if they are as normal as could be. We might dismiss this as being a happenstance of history, but it happens all the time in our modern age, too. Stories about men such as Harvey Weinstein, Jeffrey Epstein, Peter Nygard, and too many others remind us that sexual exploitation of women by men in power is an everyday occurrence. The abuse of power that is embodied here in the sexual act can cause us to recoil, and yet it is too often excused as a case of "boys will be boys," or "they can't help it."

I once heard a woman say, with regards to Bathsheba, "She seduced the king. She knew he'd be watching and she purposely bathed on the roof to tempt him. Poor man." The group I was a part of gently and firmly tried to spell out some of the dynamics that were far more likely to have been at play. But it's also worth pointing out that the woman's comment reflects an earlier, inaccurate rendering of the Hebrew text. This inaccuracy has been corrected in most modern translations, like the one above, where it is clear that it is not *Bathsheba* who is on the roof, but *David* who is on the roof of the palace looking down on her. This is what the original Hebrew text *actually* says. Bathsheba may have been outside, most likely within the walled courtyard of her home, but this would not have been unusual for the time.

BIBLE STUDY

HEBREW
SCRIPTURES
Women in the Bible
FOR
Progressive
Christians

When the king's men come to take her, Bathsheba has no choice but to go with them. She and David may not even have exchanged any words. The reality is simple in its horror: this is a story of rape. Bathsheba is an amusing plaything for David, nothing more or less.

Once Bathsheba realizes she is pregnant, the account solidifies as a man's story. Rather than give us any insight into her feelings, the remainder of the narrative tells us of how David tries a number of sneaky maneuvers to avoid being found out. When they fail, he arranges to have Bathsheba's husband killed. Again, her feelings are not entertained by David, and the narrative tells us only that she mourned her husband, Uriah. When that official mourning period was over, David sent for her again, and married her. She had a baby boy, then basically fades into the woodwork until after the death of their first child, when David "comforts" her and they go on to have a second son named Solomon.

This is a key and illustrative story, because it reminds us of how women – even when they should be the central character of a narrative – get pushed aside in favour of the men. Even when Bathsheba is "remembered" in the genealogy of Jesus (Matthew 1:1-16), her name is omitted, and she is only referred to as the woman who "had been the wife of Uriah." She is an "also-ran" in her own traumatic story.

Such is the reality of too many women throughout history.

Vashti

If Bathsheba's story gets lost in the story of a man (King David), Queen Vashti's story, which appears in the book of Esther, tends to get pushed behind the larger story of Queen Esther, which we will explore in the next session. Yet Vashti's story is more than a mere tool to set up the arrival of Esther; Vashti's brief appearance on history's stage shows us that when a woman stands up for herself it can have powerful effect.

Not everyone has been happy that the book of Esther made it into the Bible. For some, the lack of any mention of God is a problem; for others it is the story itself. Martin Luther, while recognizing that he could not get rid of the book because it was a part of the Hebrew scriptures, nonetheless wished the book did not exist because it was too Jewish and full of "pagan naughtiness."[3] It may also be that the book has met resistance because it contains the stories of two women – Vashti and Esther – who act in strong, defiant, and powerful ways, in contrast to the men around them, and who cause serious discomfort for those men, who think they are in charge but who seem to lack the strength of their own convictions. This, in fact, may be the real point of the book: women (like men) can be powerful and courageous, and can stand up to men in ways that have far-reaching and long-lasting effects. Given our modern perspective, we might think we already know this, but it's worth noting how often we're surprised when a woman "succeeds," especially in what we might have thought was a male realm.

The events described in the book of Esther ostensibly take place during the reign of King Xerxes (referred to in most versions as King Ahasuerus, a word that sounds like the Hebrew word for headache). Xerxes ruled in the Achaemenid Empire, or modern-day Iran, from the years 486 to 465 BCE. The story in Esther, however, is heavily fictionalized – a stance supported by the fact that, with the exception of the king, none of the key characters (Esther, Vashti, Mordecai, or Haman) appear in other historical accounts. The story overflows with exaggeration. It also begins with the Hebrew expression, "In those days ..." (1:2), which some see as being akin to the English, "Once upon a time ..."

> **BIBLE STUDY**
> HEBREW SCRIPTURES
> **Women in the Bible**
> FOR Progressive Christians

> **Fiction is not the *absence* of truth, but often the *vehicle* for it.**
> – Carol M. Bechtel, *Esther*

Esther 1:1–22

This is what happened back when Ahasuerus lived, the very Ahasuerus who ruled from India to Cush – one hundred twenty-seven provinces in all. ²At that time, Ahasuerus ruled the kingdom from his royal throne in the fortified part of Susa. ³In the third year of his rule he hosted a feast for all his officials and courtiers. The leaders of Persia and Media attended, along with his provincial officials and officers. ⁴He showed off the awesome riches of his kingdom and beautiful treasures as mirrors of how very great he was. The event lasted a long time –

BIBLE STUDY

HEBREW
SCRIPTURES
**Women in
the Bible**
FOR
Progressive
Christians

six whole months, to be exact! ⁵After that the king held a seven-day feast for everyone in the fortified part of Susa. Whether they were important people in the town or not, they all met in the walled garden of the royal palace. ⁶White linen curtains and purple hangings were held up by shining white and red-purple ropes tied to silver rings and marble posts. Gold and silver couches sat on a mosaic floor made of gleaming purple crystal, marble, and mother-of-pearl. ⁷They served the drinks in cups made of gold, and each cup was different. The king made sure there was plenty of royal wine. ⁸The rule about the drinks was "No limits!" The king had ordered everyone serving wine in the palace to offer as much as each guest wanted. ⁹At the same time, Queen Vashti held a feast for women in King Ahasuerus' palace.

¹⁰On the seventh day, when wine had put the king in high spirits, he gave an order to Mehuman, Biztha, Harbona, Bigtha, Abagtha, Zethar, and Carcas, the seven eunuchs who served King Ahasuerus personally. ¹¹They were to bring Queen Vashti before him wearing the royal crown. She was gorgeous, and he wanted to show off her beauty both to the general public and to his important guests. ¹²But Queen Vashti refused to come as the king had ordered through the eunuchs. The king was furious, his anger boiling inside. ¹³Now, when a need arose, the king would often talk with certain very smart people about the best way to handle it. They were people who knew both the kingdom's written laws and what judges had decided about cases in the past. ¹⁴The ones he talked with most often were Carshena, Shethar, Admatha, Tarshish, Meres, Marsena, and Memucan. They were seven very important people in Persia and Media who, as the kingdom's highest leaders, were in the king's inner circle. So the king said to them, ¹⁵"According to the law, what should I do with Queen Vashti since she didn't do what King Ahasuerus ordered her through the eunuchs?"

¹⁶Then Memucan spoke up in front of the king and the officials. "Queen Vashti," he said, "has done something wrong not just to the king himself. She has also done wrong to all the officials and the peoples in all the provinces of King Ahasuerus. ¹⁷This is the reason: News of what the queen did will reach all women, making them look down on their husbands. They will say, 'King Ahasuerus ordered servants to bring Queen Vashti before him, but she refused to come.' ¹⁸This very day, the

important women of Persia and Media who hear about the queen will tell the royal officials the same thing. There will be no end of put-downs and arguments. [19]Now, if the king wishes, let him send out a royal order and have it written into the laws of Persia and Media, laws no one can ever change. It should say that Vashti will never again come before King Ahasuerus. It should also say that the king will give her royal place to someone better than she. [20]When the order becomes public through the whole empire, vast as it is, all women will treat their husbands properly. The rule should touch everyone, whether from an important family or not."

[21]The king liked the plan, as did the other men, and he did just what Memucan said. [22]He sent written orders to all the king's provinces. Each province received it written in its own alphabet and each people received it in its own language. It said that each husband should rule over his own house.

Right off the bat the story is larger than life. There are simply no records of any empire possessing 127 provinces, and we know from other historical records that the Achaemenid Empire had between 20 and 30 provinces. This should remind us that in many ways we are reading what might be described as a "fish story" – the basic facts are real, but the story has been added to and massaged to make the fish larger and the act of catching it all the more dramatic. Another example of exaggeration occurs in verse 4, when we read that the party the king hosted lasted for six months – really?! – and the wine flowed without limit.

As if the author knows the reader will be questioning the veracity of the story right out of the gate, verse 6 provides an inordinate amount of detail, including how the curtains were held up, and the lavish description of the crystal, marble, and mother-of-pearl floor. Clearly, all of this is intended to give us the impression that Ahasuerus is wealthy beyond comprehension. In a world where wealth equalled power, this is in turn a way of saying that this king held more power than the rest of the world combined – or at least so it seemed. After several verses describing the king's "feast" in elaborate detail, the feast held by Queen Vashti for the women is mentioned almost as a mere afterthought in verse 9.

BIBLE STUDY

HEBREW SCRIPTURES
Women in the Bible
FOR
Progressive Christians

Like the exquisite detail in verses 6 and 7, the mention of the names of the eunuchs in verse 10 is a writer's device to indicate that this is a factual story, though we have no other sources against which to test these names. As one commentator stated, all this really proves is that the author knew some Persian names.

The story of Queen Vashti really takes off in verse 11. When he is quite drunk, the king asks the queen to parade before the men at his party, who are also presumably quite drunk. The request for her to wear the royal crown has generally been understood to mean he wanted her to wear nothing else. This was certainly the understanding of the ancient rabbis who discussed this story, and they further added the detail that the king had a habit of paying prostitutes to parade naked in front of him when he was younger; thus, he is treating the queen here as a prostitute – a horrific disgrace to her majesty, to the fact that she is his wife, and to her simple dignity as a person.

Verse 12 contains the pivotal words, "But Queen Vashti refused ..." The king's response – boiling in anger – is hardly surprising, especially given his drunkenness. What follows is a lengthy discussion about how the king should respond. Again, several details are added, including the names of the advisors, to give the story more weight. It soon becomes apparent that the issue is not so much that Vashti refused a royal edict, but rather that word of her disobedience might leak out to the other women of the kingdom, who might then also refuse to obey their husbands. This, the men determine, simply cannot be risked or tolerated. The decision is made to banish Queen Vashti and to replace her with another woman. This would ensure, verse 20 tells us, that women would treat their husbands "properly."

This order is sent to all the provinces of the empire. Lest anyone misunderstand it, it is written in the alphabets and languages of each province. The order decrees that "each husband should rule over his own house." Thus, order is maintained, and the stage is set for a new queen – presumably one who will obey the king in all matters.

The story offers the intriguing juxtaposition of Queen Vashti, who says "no," and the men, who stumble over one another in a panic about what to do when a woman stands up for herself or refuses to obey her husband.

Vashti, of course has the right to say no to any request, let alone one as insulting and degrading as the king's demand that she dance naked before a bunch of drunken men. Clearly, throughout the story, Vashti is the one who exhibits strength while the men exhibit cowardice and panic. She has turned the tables on an abusive situation and has exerted her identity.

Questions

■ Why do you think the stories of Bathsheba and Vashti were preserved? What might the respective authors be wanting us to take from them?

■ How are these women similar to – or different from – other women in the Bible?

■ Do you consider the story of Bathsheba to be one of rape, seduction, abuse of power, or something else?

■ Try to imagine the relationship between Bathsheba and King David – at the beginning, after the death of Bathsheba's husband, and later in life. What might it have been like?

■ God is not mentioned by name in the book of Esther. How important is it to you that God be included in a biblical book?

■ How do you feel when reading history that has been "augmented" – that is, when you can tell some of the facts have been exaggerated to make the story grander? Does this weaken the message or enhance it? Do you have the same feeling when watching a movie or television program?

■ How important to you is the factual accuracy, or historicity, of the story of Vashti – or of any biblical story?

■ The issue of wives "obeying" their husbands is central to Queen Vashti's story. Notice that it is the men who decide, from a stance of fear, what must be done. What might be some of the fallout if women stopped obeying their husbands?

- What do you make of the fear of the men?
- Scholar Carol M. Bechtel, in her commentary on Esther in the *Interpretation* series, notes that "the character of Vashti has long fascinated feminists and frightened misogynists" (p. 11). How do you respond to that statement?
- Do some imagining about Vashti. What do you think might have happened to her after she was banished?

SESSION 3

Women Who Are Survivors: Tamar and Esther

The previous session introduced Queen Vashti and the book of Esther. In this session we will explore the story of Esther herself. It is a powerful story of a woman who finds ways to survive in a difficult situation, and who saves her people from annihilation in the process. However, before we meet Esther let us look briefly at the story of Tamar.

Tamar

The story of Tamar is found in Genesis 38 and in some ways interrupts the story of Joseph and his siblings. That fact alone makes it intriguing. Why would a story such as this interrupt one of the longest and arguably most important narratives in scripture? Obviously, someone thought it was worth sharing and exploring here.

To summarize the story, Judah's son Er married a woman called Tamar, but Er died before they had any children. At the time, there was a law known as Levirate marriage, which dictated that if a man died without leaving any children his brother should marry the man's widow, sleep with her, and hopefully produce a child who would legally be the descendant of the deceased man. According to this law, when Er died his brother Shelah should have slept with Tamar and tried to have a child by her. This child would then have inherited Er's estate. But Judah, Tamar's father-in-law, does not allow either of his sons to sleep with her. Not only does this prevent the deceased son Er from leaving a descendant, but it renders Tamar a non-person, because she was not legally attached to a father, husband, or son. Tamar might have disappeared from the story altogether, but instead she decides to assert her rights.

When she learns that Judah is coming to town, she dresses up as a prostitute and sits by the roadside. Judah decides to sleep

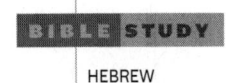

HEBREW SCRIPTURES
Women in the Bible
FOR Progressive Christians

with her, having no idea who she is. As payment, he leaves his seal and staff with her. And, of course, she becomes pregnant.

When news of the pregnancy reaches Judah, he is furious – Tamar has slept with a man! She should be put to death! Tamar is brought to Judah and says coyly, "I'm pregnant by the man to whom these things belong" and she shows his seal and staff – which would be like producing his wallet and driver's licence today. Judah realizes he has been caught out and declares, "she's more righteous than I am." Tamar has her child – twins, in fact – and everyone lives happily ever after.

Is Tamar a sly woman who simply uses sex to get what she wants? Or is she a clever woman who uses one of the few things available to her to get what she deserves under the law? Does she take advantage of Judah, or simply force him to live up to his family obligations?

Tamar's story is an intriguing story on several levels. It reminds us that while women often have limited means, they often also have the strength to stand up for themselves and their rights, regardless of how men treat them. They have as much right to survive as men do and must not be looked down upon for exerting that right.

Esther

The book of Esther is read in its entirety every year at the Jewish festival of Purim. The story is used as burlesque, a sad caricature of the silliness (at best) of those who try to put down other nations or groups. Many see here a wonderful parable of the negative outcome that inevitably awaits anyone who seeks to write off a group of people based on their nationality, culture, language, practices, sexuality, or other features to which they have an inherent and God-given right. Thus, the book is far more than a simple story of events in the history of the Jewish people.

Unfortunately for Christian churches that follow the lectionary, the book of Esther appears only once in the *Revised Common Lectionary*, and even then only a handful of verses are read that tell the barest hint of the story and none of the intrigue. For that reason, many people are quite unaware of this powerful story.

To really appreciate everything this amazing book has to offer, one needs to read it from start to finish, preferably in one sitting. (It's only about eight to ten pages in the average English-language Bible.) By reading it this way, one encounters all the elements and nuances that make for a great story, and that tell us much about the situation of the Jews not just during the Achaemenid Empire, but throughout much of history. (I suggest that you take a break here and read the entire book of Esther, if you haven't already done so, before continuing with the rest of the session.)

Like Tamar's story, Esther's story is also one of survival, although it does not initially dawn on her that her life is in danger, or that she can do anything about it. However, she comes to realize that she holds an amazing amount of power, and she uses it in an awesome way.

Given the length of the book of Esther, some of the text will be included in this session, and for other portions I will offer a brief summary, which will appear in square brackets.

Esther 2:1–20

[When the king's anger over Queen Vashti's refusal finally subsided, some of his advisors suggested the king search for the most beautiful woman in the kingdom to become his new wife. He thought it was a great idea, and so the process began.]

⁵Now there was a Jew in the fortified part of Susa whose name was Mordecai, Jair's son. He came from the family line of Shimei and Kish; he was a Benjaminite. (⁶Benjaminites had been taken into exile away from Jerusalem along with the group, which included Judah's King Jeconiah, whom Babylon's King Nebuchadnezzar exiled to Babylon.) ⁷Mordecai had been a father to Hadassah (that is, Esther), though she was really his cousin, because she had neither father nor mother. The girl had a beautiful figure and was lovely to look at. When her parents died, Mordecai had taken her to be his daughter. ⁸When the king's order and his new law became public, many young women were gathered into the fortified part of Susa under the

BIBLE STUDY

HEBREW
SCRIPTURES
Women in the Bible
FOR
Progressive
Christians

care of Hegai. Esther was also taken to the palace to the care of Hegai, the one in charge of the women. ⁹The young woman pleased him and won his kindness. He quickly began her beauty treatments and gave her carefully chosen foods. He also gave her seven servants selected from among the palace servants and moved her and her servants into the nicest rooms in the women's house. (¹⁰Esther hadn't told anyone her race and family background because Mordecai had ordered her not to.) ¹¹Each day found Mordecai pacing back and forth along the wall in front of the women's house to learn how Esther was doing and what they were doing with her. ¹²According to the rules for women, the moment for each young woman to go to King Ahasuerus came at the end of twelve months. (She had six months of treatment with pleasant-smelling creams and six months with fragrant oils and other treatments for women.) ¹³So this is how the young woman would go to the king: They gave her anything that she asked to take with her from the women's house to the palace. ¹⁴In the evening she would go in, and the next morning she would return to the second women's house under the care of Shaashgaz. He was the king's eunuch in charge of the secondary wives. She would never go to the king again unless he was so pleased that he called for her by name. ¹⁵Soon the moment came for Esther daughter of Mordecai's uncle Abihail, whom Mordecai had taken as his own daughter, to go to the king. But she asked for nothing except what Hegai the king's eunuch in charge of the women told her. (Esther kept winning the favor of everyone who saw her.)

¹⁶Esther was taken to King Ahasuerus, to his own palace, in the tenth month (that is, the month of Tevet) in the seventh year of his rule. ¹⁷The king loved Esther more than all the other women; she had won his love and his favor more than all the others. He placed the royal crown on her head and made her ruler in place of Vashti. ¹⁸The king held a magnificent, lavish feast, "the feast of Esther," for all his officials and courtiers. He declared a public holiday for the provinces and gave out gifts with royal generosity. ¹⁹When they gathered the young women to the second women's house, Mordecai was working for the king at the King's Gate. ²⁰Esther still wasn't telling anyone her family background and race, just as Mordecai had ordered her. She continued to do what Mordecai said, just as she did when she was in his care.

Verse 6, which almost feels like a footnote, is important because it shows a link between the Benjaminites (along with other Jews) who were taken against their will into captivity in Babylon, and what happens to Esther and countless other women who are taken against their will. In other words, while Esther is about to gain a lot of wealth and power, she is nonetheless a prisoner in the larger context of the situation.

Mordecai, who will be a key figure in the story, adopts his orphaned niece who appears to have two names: Esther and Hadassah. It has been suggested that Hadassah is a Hebrew translation of Esther (both names mean myrtle wood). However, the names Esther and Mordecai are considered by some to be too similar to the Babylonian deities Ishtar and Marduk to be overlooked, suggesting that this story has been adapted to a Jewish context from an older Babylonian myth.

Esther is one of the women chosen for the king to "try" – there really isn't a more polite way to put it. The women go through a year's beauty regimen (remember that exaggeration is a key feature of this entire story) and then spend a night with the king. Based on his experience, one of them will be chosen queen. On the advice of her relative, Mordecai, Esther hides the fact that she his Jewish. When it is eventually her turn to sleep with the king, he is so impressed he immediately crowns Esther as the new queen.

Esther 2:21–23

21At that time, as Mordecai continued to work at the King's Gate, two royal eunuchs, Bigthan and Teresh, became angry with King Ahasuerus. They were among the guards protecting the doorway to the king, but they secretly planned to kill him. 22When Mordecai got wind of it, he reported it to Queen Esther. She spoke to the king about it, saying the information came from Mordecai. 23The matter was investigated and found to be true, so the two men were impaled on pointed poles. A report about the event was written in the royal record with the king present.

BIBLE STUDY

HEBREW
SCRIPTURES
Women in the Bible
FOR
Progressive
Christians

If the story of Esther were a miniseries, the first episode about Queen Esther would end with this small – but highly significant – tidbit. Mordecai learns of a plot to kill the king and tells Queen Esther. She in turn tells the king about it, and – very importantly, as we see later – it is written down in front of the king.

Mordecai and Haman

A key element of the story of Esther surrounds the relationship between her relative and foster father Mordecai, and the king's rather reprehensible chief of staff. There is something behind their relationship that festers throughout the story until, for Haman, it boils over with disastrous results.

Haman is named as being "son of Hammedatha the Agagite" and Mordecai, we are told, is of the Jewish tribe of Benjamin, which puts Mordecai in the family of the late King Saul. Back in 1 Samuel 15 we read that Saul did not execute Agag and, because of that, Saul's reign was doomed. Accordingly, the Benjaminites and the Agagites have no use for each other. Knowing this, it comes as no surprise that Mordecai refuses to bow to Haman, and conversely Haman would be especially incensed that Mordecai does not bow to him. The infamous story of the Hatfields and McCoys comes to mind, the saga of two families that fought furiously. Many will recall former U.S. President Donald Trump's irrational and unfounded rant about the election in 2020 having been fraudulently stolen from him, and this seems to have some parallels in the incredibly negative attitude Haman displays toward Mordecai. He does not merely dislike him – he abjectly despises him.

Esther 3 – 5:8

[The King promotes Haman to the position of prime minister and everyone now has to bow to Haman. Mordecai refuses – perhaps because he despises Haman's heritage, perhaps because he thought he should have been promoted; the text is ambiguous. Haman is outraged and decides to eliminate not just Mordecai (a Jew) but to kill all the Jews in the realm.

The King's servants throw *purim*, or lots, to choose a day for the annihilation of the Jews.

Haman then tells the king that there is a "certain group" rampant through all the provinces – implying they have somehow infiltrated everywhere – and they do not obey the king's laws. He offers a large payment if the king will grant him permission to wipe them out, and the king agrees. An order goes out to the entire realm, written in the various languages and alphabets of the people there, ordering them to kill all the Jews – men, women, children – on the 13th day of the month of Adar.

When Mordecai finds out about the plot, he tears his clothes and puts ashes on his head – typical signs of mourning or lamentation – and goes to the King's Gate. Meanwhile, all the Jews get word of the fate that is to befall them, roughly a year in the future, and cry out throughout the land.

Esther learns that Mordecai is in mourning but does not know why. She sends him some new clothes (which he rejects) and then sends a messenger named Hathach to find out what's going on. Mordecai tells Hathach about the Jews' pending destruction, and Hathach reports it all to the queen.]

4*¹⁰In reply Esther ordered Hathach to tell Mordecai: ¹¹"All the king's officials and the people in his provinces know that there's a single law in a case like this. Any man or woman who comes to the king in the inner courtyard without being called is to be put to death. Only the person to whom the king holds out the gold scepter may live. In my case, I haven't been called to come to the king for the past thirty days."*

¹²When they told Mordecai Esther's words, ¹³he had them respond to Esther: "Don't think for one minute that, unlike all the other Jews, you'll come out of this alive simply because you are in the palace. ¹⁴In fact, if you don't speak up at this very important time, relief and rescue will appear for the Jews from another place, but you and your family will die. But who knows? Maybe it was for a moment like this that you came to be part of the royal family."

¹⁵Esther sent back this word to Mordecai: ¹⁶"Go, gather all the Jews who are in Susa and tell them to give up eating to help me be brave. They aren't to eat or drink anything for three whole days, and I myself will do the same, along with my

BIBLE STUDY

HEBREW
SCRIPTURES
**Women in
the Bible**
FOR
Progressive
Christians

BIBLE STUDY

HEBREW
SCRIPTURES
Women in the Bible
FOR
Progressive
Christians

Coincidence is the pseudonym dear God chooses when he wants to remain incognito.
– Albert Schweitzer

---

female servants. Then, even though it's against the law, I will go to the king; and if I am to die, then die I will." ¹⁷So Mordecai left where he was and did exactly what Esther had ordered him.

5¹Three days later, Esther put on royal clothes and stood in the inner courtyard of the palace, facing the palace itself. At that moment the king was inside sitting on his royal throne and facing the palace doorway. ²When the king noticed Queen Esther standing in the entry court, he was pleased. The king held out to Esther the gold scepter in his hand, and she came forward and touched the scepter's tip.

³Then the king said to her, "What is it, Queen Esther? What do you want? I'll give you anything – even half the kingdom."

⁴Esther answered, "If the king wishes, please come today with Haman for the feast that I have prepared for him."

⁵"Hurry, get Haman," the king ordered, "so we can do what Esther says." So the king and Haman came to the feast that Esther had prepared. ⁶As they sipped wine, the king asked, "Now what is it you wish? I'll give it to you. What do you want? I'll do anything – even give you half the kingdom."

⁷Esther answered, "This is my wish and this is what I want: ⁸If I please the king, and if the king wishes to grant my wish and my desire, I'd like the king and Haman to come to another feast that I will prepare for them. Tomorrow I will answer the king's questions."

We are reminded here that this is a typical royal household in those times: the king rules, and the queen is clearly secondary. No one, not even the queen, is allowed to enter the king's presence without being summoned and thus Esther believes she can do nothing. Mordecai's response is strong and powerful. "Don't think you'll escape this destruction," he tells her. And here he utters his most important line, *"But – maybe it was for a moment like this that you became queen."*

Esther calls upon the Jews in Susa (the capital city) to fast for three days – this is a traditional Jewish form of prayer, or of getting God's attention and requesting assistance. Esther promises that she and her servants will do the same, and then she will approach the king.

43

BIBLE STUDY

HEBREW SCRIPTURES
Women in the Bible
FOR
Progressive Christians

The king's offer to give Esther half the kingdom – given first in 5:3, again in 5:6 and again in 7:2 – indicates his infatuation and admiration of her. Esther's plot unfolds slowly and methodically. She shows the king and Haman a great time at a sumptuous banquet, and then at the end invites them to another.

Esther 5:9 – 7:10

[Haman leaves the palace in a happy mood only to have it come crashing down when he sees Mordecai who brushes him off, leaving Haman feeling "great rage" toward Mordecai. He goes home and boasts about how much the king has honoured him, and how he is invited to another banquet the next night. Yet he offers that this is worthless whenever he sees Mordecai's face.

His wife and friends suggest preparing a 75-foot (23 metre) tall, sharpened pole with the intent of impaling Mordecai on it.

Meanwhile, the king cannot sleep and invites his servants to read the royal records to him. They come to the part about Mordecai saving him, and the king realizes he never repaid him properly. He notices Haman outside and has him brought in.

"What should I do to honour someone?" the king asks, and Haman assumes the king is referring to him. Haman offers some suggestions. When Haman is finished, the king says, "Go and do all this for Mordecai the Jew." You can imagine Haman's reaction. He has no choice. He does what the king has commanded, and then goes home to his wife and tells her everything. She tells him he's losing out to Mordecai and, in an intriguing statement, points out that if he is Jewish then Haman cannot win against him.]

7:1 When the king and Haman came in for the banquet with Queen Esther, 2the king said to her, "This is the second day we've met for wine. What is your wish, Queen Esther? I'll give it to you. And what do you want? I'll do anything – even give you half the kingdom."

3Queen Esther answered, "If I please the king, and if the king wishes, give me my life – that's my wish – and the lives of my people too. That's my desire. 4We have been sold – I and my people – to be wiped out, killed, and destroyed. If we simply had

BIBLE STUDY

HEBREW
SCRIPTURES
Women in the Bible
FOR
Progressive
Christians

been sold as male and female slaves, I would have said nothing. But no enemy can compensate the king for this kind of damage."

⁵King Ahasuerus said to Queen Esther, "Who is this person, and where is he? Who would dare do such a thing?"

⁶Esther replied, "A man who hates, an enemy – this wicked Haman!" Haman was overcome with terror in the presence of the king and queen. ⁷Furious, the king got up and left the banquet for the palace garden. But Haman stood up to beg Queen Esther for his life. He saw clearly that the king's mood meant a bad end for him.

⁸The king returned from the palace garden to the banquet room just as Haman was kneeling on the couch where Esther was reclining. "Will you even molest the queen while I am in the house?" the king said. The words had barely left the king's mouth before covering Haman's face with dread.

⁹Harbona, one of the eunuchs serving the king, said, "Sir, look! There's the stake that Haman made for Mordecai, the man who spoke up and did something good for the king. It's standing at Haman's house – seventy-five feet high."

"Impale him on it!" the king ordered. ¹⁰So they impaled Haman on the very pole that he had set up for Mordecai, and the king's anger went away.

Esther states her simple request: save me and my people. At the same time, she has taken the huge leap of identifying herself as a Jew. She also says, essentially, "If we were only going to be sold into slavery, I wouldn't have bothered you, but if we are killed you'll lose this massive labour force and it will have huge economic implications."

When the king asks who on earth would plot something as heinous as this genocide, Esther's description of Haman is accurate and stinging. Who is doing this? "A man who hates," she replies. Then, in a "too good to be true" moment, Haman is kneeling in front of the queen, who is reclining on a couch, at the very moment the king storms back into the room. He puts two and two together (wrongly in this case) and assumes Haman is trying to take advantage of the queen.

Clearly a sense of "we need a good story no matter what" comes into play again, as it seems just a little too convenient that the huge pole (meant for Mordecai) is standing right outside, and thus the obvious solution to everything is to impale Haman on it. Done and dusted.

Esther 8:1 – 10:3

[With Haman out of the way, a problem still remains: what to do about the edict requiring the extermination of the Jews. Esther asks the king, "How can I watch others destroy my own family?"

Apparently, the king's orders cannot be rescinded, not even by the king himself! However, Ahasuerus is able to issue a new edict warning the Jews of pending annihilation and allowing them to arm themselves and fight back. This edict goes everywhere, in multiple languages and alphabets, just like the first edict. In essence, the Jews are given licence to destroy all who would attack them – a kind of pre-emptive revenge in its fullest flower. We are even told at the very end of chapter 8 that many people throughout the land "became Jews" so as to avoid their own destruction.

On the appointed day, the Jews are attacked, they fight back and, to no one's surprise, win a resounding victory. We are told they do not take any booty; there is some more fighting, and then it stops. Esther and Mordecai issue decrees to make sure that all the Jews observe the festival of Purim for all eternity. The book wraps up with a note that the king's deeds are many and dutifully written down, and that Mordecai remained a good guy to the end. Esther essentially disappears now that her work is done.]

The ending of the book adds to the difficulty the rest of it presents: Esther, a Jewish woman, is set in place for a specific task, which she executes with great finesse, but otherwise she is not mentioned much. Perhaps this is not surprising given that the book is written by a man in a very sexist time. Yet the truth is that only a queen could have influenced the king the way in which Esther did, and only an exceptional woman could become a queen in the style of Esther in the first place. What she does in this story is pivotal to the survival of the Jewish nation, not only in the time told of in the book, but throughout history since. It is no wonder

BIBLE STUDY

HEBREW SCRIPTURES
Women in the Bible
FOR
Progressive Christians

> Esther is a literary masterpiece: what makes it so is the weaving together, with supreme economy, of a series of small coincidences into one large, fortunate coincidence.
> – Emil Fackenheim

that the Nazis would not permit this book to be read during the Third Reich – its message of saving the Jews from annihilation is a potent one for sure.

Questions

■ Why do you think the stories of Tamar and Esther were preserved? What might the authors be wanting us to take from them?

■ How are these women similar to – or different from – other women in the Bible?

■ Tamar intentionally disguises herself and seduces her father-in-law. What is your reaction to this story?

■ The issue of Levirate marriage benefitted deceased men (by potentially giving them a male heir) and living women (by giving them a potential man/son to care for them and ensure their survival). What do you think of this system? Who benefits the most?

■ Some people have argued that Esther merely plays along with patriarchy, even giving in to it. Others point out that, in those days and within that culture, she really had no choice. What do you think?

■ Mordecai tells Esther that perhaps she became queen just for this moment, for the chance to intervene. When do you think things have happened to set you in the right place at the right time? To what extent do you think God was involved in that?

■ The Jews call the reading of this book and its related celebration "Purim," which refers to the lots cast to determine a date for their annihilation. Some say there is great power in claiming a negative term as a positive in such a situation – similar to the way the LGBTQ community embraced the word "queer" to describe themselves. What do you think?

■ When Haman reports to the king about the "need" to eliminate the Jews, he uses inflammatory language, describing them as a group of people who infiltrated every nook and cranny of the kingdom. What are other situations are you aware of when similar kinds of language have been used? What were the consequences? How might we combat them?

- What are the consequences of holding a grudge?
- Most people have probably heard the expression, "Hell hath no fury like a woman scorned." Yet the person exhibiting the most astonishing and hate-filled anger in this story is a man. What do you think is served by labelling a group of people with a specific trait, such as astonishing anger?
- Mordecai tells Esther that she may well have become queen for just "such a time as this." Name other women whose lives seem to be set in their time.
- Why might the Nazis have banned the reading of this book during the Third Reich? To what extent do you consider the story to be subversive?

SESSION 4

Women Who Are Outsiders: Rahab and Ruth

The story the Hebrew scriptures tell is primarily one of God's favour upon the Jewish nation and people, often at the expense of others. Thus, whenever a Gentile – that is, a non-Jew – is seen as being of worth and benefit, the story stands out. When said person is also a woman, the story is all the more memorable. In this session we will look at two such persons – Rahab and Ruth – and notice how their stories are presented.

Rahab

The story of Rahab appears in Joshua 2. When the Jews were preparing to enter and take over Jericho, Joshua sent two men, two spies, into Jericho on a reconnaissance mission; we are told they went to the home of a prostitute named Rahab, where they "bedded down" – read into that last phrase all you wish. The king of Jericho sends messengers to Rahab looking for the men, but she lies and says, "They were here, but they left. Hurry, they went that way – you might catch them!" When the king's men leave the city, they are locked out.

Rahab then summons the two spies who she has hidden in the back of her house and tells them she knows they have been sent by God. "Remember I have been loyal to you," she says, "and spare me and my family when you conquer this land." The men agree, she helps them escape, and later they ensure her family's survival when the Jews invade.

It is intriguing that the biblical story makes no fuss about the fact that Rahab is a prostitute, nor about the fact that the two Hebrew soldiers spent the night at her home. This is a clue to us that prostitution was not necessarily seen as a negative thing in that culture – yet it has been seen as a huge issue throughout Jewish and Christian history. The celebration of a prostitute and a foreigner as an ancestor of Jesus (she appears in his genealogy in Matthew 1:1–16) and as a person of the faith is unusual and has raised more than a few eyebrows over the years.

The ancient rabbis struggled with the fact that Rahab was a prostitute, some of them going so far as to suggest that she was really just an innkeeper. Yet the scriptures refer to her as a prostitute and seem to have no difficulty doing so. She has been remembered that way centuries later and the overall implication is that this simply was not and is not an issue.

Rahab is mentioned in Christian scriptures in a few places – notably in Hebrews 11:31: "By faith Rahab the prostitute wasn't killed with the disobedient because she welcomed the spies in peace." In James 2:25 we read, "Wasn't Rahab the prostitute shown to be righteous when she received the messengers as her guest and then sent them on by another road?" She is simply praised for her courageous act and is not singled out for her foreign status or her choice of profession. This is key, because we tend to look at such stories and impose upon them layers of judgment from the present era, judgment which did not exist in biblical times.

Ruth

The book of Ruth is probably a work of fiction, written at a key time in Israelite history. The book is set, we are told in the first verse, in the time of the judges. However, most scholars believe it was written some time later – probably at the time the Jews returned from exile in Babylon. This is about 550 years after King David (who figures at the end of Ruth's story) and there is a great deal of evidence in the language used in the book to support this.

Not coincidentally, this was a time when the law decreed that Jewish men should divorce their non-Jewish wives (see Ezra 9–10, and Nehemiah 10:28–30). The idea that the book was written during this time, and in response to this situation, is supported by the vast majority of scholars, and, in truth, the book serves little purpose otherwise. In stark contrast to the Jewish law at the time, which saw foreign wives as "disposable," the book of Ruth presents them as human beings, worthy of love and dignity.

We don't know who wrote the book of Ruth, and so also don't know whether it was written by a man or a woman. An argument can be made that Ruth originated with one or more women, at least within the oral tradition. This idea is supported by the fact that the story is told from a female perspective, which differs from that of male authors at the time. It's generally assumed that male authors would not have been this sensitive. Quite possibly the story was at least first told by women and over time was written down by someone who wanted to maintain some of its earliest form.

In the interests of space and time I shall include parts of the story directly from the Bible, and at other times will offer a brief summary.

Ruth 1:1–22

[There was a famine in the land, so a man from Bethlehem took his wife Naomi, and their two sons, and moved to the land of Moab. The man died, and over time the two sons married Moabite women, Orpah and Ruth. Later, both sons died without any children, leaving Naomi with no husband or sons. Naomi learned that the famine had ended, and so she decided to return to Bethlehem.]

⁸Naomi said to her daughters-in-law, "Go, turn back, each of you to the household of your mother. May the Lord deal faithfully with you, just as you have done with the dead and with me. ⁹May the Lord provide for you so that you may find security, each woman in the household of her husband." Then she kissed them, and they lifted up their voices and wept.

¹⁰But they replied to her, "No, instead we will return with you, to your people."

¹¹Naomi replied, "Turn back, my daughters. Why would you go with me? Will there again be sons in my womb, that they would be husbands for you? ¹²Turn back, my daughters. Go. I am too old for a husband. If I were to say that I have hope, even if I had a husband tonight, and even more, if I were to bear sons – ¹³would you wait until they grew up? Would you refrain from having a husband? No, my daughters. This is more bitter for me than for you, since the Lord's will has come out against me."

14Then they lifted up their voices and wept again. Orpah kissed her mother-in-law, but Ruth stayed with her. 15Naomi said, "Look, your sister-in-law is returning to her people and to her gods. Turn back after your sister-in-law."

16But Ruth replied, "Don't urge me to abandon you, to turn back from following after you. Wherever you go, I will go; and wherever you stay, I will stay. Your people will be my people, and your God will be my God. 17Wherever you die, I will die, and there I will be buried. May the Lord do this to me and more so if even death separates me from you." 18When Naomi saw that Ruth was determined to go with her, she stopped speaking to her about it.

19So both of them went along until they arrived at Bethlehem. When they arrived at Bethlehem, the whole town was excited on account of them, and the women of the town asked, "Can this be Naomi?"

20She replied to them, "Don't call me Naomi [Pleasant], but call me Mara [Bitter], for the Almighty [El Shaddai] has made me very bitter. 21I went away full, but the Lord has returned me empty. Why would you call me Naomi, when the Lord has testified against me, and the Almighty has deemed me guilty?"

22Thus Naomi returned. And Ruth the Moabite, her daughter-in-law, returned with her from the territory of Moab. They arrived in Bethlehem at the beginning of the barley harvest.

One may or may not recall that Moab was presented as a "bad place" in the book of Numbers: some Jewish men had slept with some Moabite women and were convinced to worship Moabite gods (Numbers 25:1-2); the king of Moab arranged to destroy Israel (chapters 22-24); and Moab was among the oppressors of Israel during the time of the judges (Judges 3:12ff). In short, the Jews despised the Moabites. So right off the bat, the introduction of two women from Moab and the fact that they loved and desired to be faithful to Naomi would have stirred the interest of the first people who heard this story. What good could possibly come from a story about Jews and Moabites?

The men's deaths set up the story which will now revolve around Naomi and Ruth being single women. Ruth's insistence that she will stay with her mother-in-law may well be what inspires Naomi to find Ruth a husband in Bethlehem, which, if she's successful, would return both of them to full standing in society. It is important to pause here and explore this issue a little more.

Jewish society – like most ancient societies – was patriarchal and centred around men. A woman's worth and security depended entirely on her relation to a male, typically a father, husband, son, or other male relative. If a woman had neither father, husband, nor sons, she had no standing in society and was thus extremely vulnerable. Unattached women were literally nobodies; the Bible is full of examples of such women who had no identity and no rights, who were shunned simply because they had no male relative.

Levirate marriage

Levirate marriage has been practiced, even into modern times, by societies around the world that have a strong clan structure, as was the case in ancient Israel. In these societies, it is important that property and wealth remain within the clan. There is also the issue of what will become of a widow if she has no male protector.

Levirate marriage in ancient Israel was a response to both problems. Basically, if a man died and left no children, and if he had a brother or brothers, one of them would marry the widow, thus ensuring that the deceased husband's property would remain in the clan. It was hoped that an heir for the deceased husband would be produced from the new union. There was also a clear intent that the widow be cared for.

In practice, however, like laws today, it is evident that there was a great deal of difference between what the law actually stated and how it was interpreted or understood, and how it was implemented, or not.

For example, in the wording of the actual law in Deuteronomy 25:5-10, it is clear that it only applies to "brothers who reside together in the same house," not to other male relatives of the deceased man. This means that when Tamar eventually had a child by her father-in-law, Judah, she was no longer acting or pursuing a claim within the constraints of Levirate law – yet later Judah himself declared that when she did this she was more in the right than he was, because he had not forced his son (her brother-in-law) to marry her.

Also, as most biblical stories that refer to Levirate marriage show, even though the purpose of the law was ostensibly to preserve the male's legacy (or name) and property, it was the *women* who pursed it most vigorously, which shouldn't surprise us – after all, their very lives depended on it. For their part, the men often tried to shirk their responsibilities.

All of these dynamics have led female scholar Dvora E. Weisberg to write, "Perhaps despite the Hebrew Bible's emphasis on the aim of providing a 'name' for a man who has died without children, the true goal of [L]evirate was viewed as the protection of widows, a goal more passionately valued and pursued by women than men."[4]

As for the story of Ruth, some scholars debate whether this has anything to do with Levirate marriage at all. It is clear that Ruth's pursuit of Boaz (at the urging of Naomi) and the eventual "transaction" that leads to their marriage have little to do with the law described in Deuteronomy, but perhaps more to do with a law in Leviticus 25:25, which doesn't mention widows or marriage at all, but focuses on land transactions.

Regardless, it's clear that the author of Ruth wanted people to hear in the story the *intent* of Levirate marriage, which was the provision for and protection of widows.

In light of all of this, Naomi sends Ruth and Orpah back home, "to the household of your mother," which is a curious and hardly accidental turn of phrase. The normal expression would have been "to the household of your father," – this is one of the places where a woman's perspective truly comes through.

Naomi prays that her daughters-in-law will regain security by finding a husband. Naomi knows the reality in which they live, and that the only way a woman can survive in that world is to be "attached" to a man.

BIBLE STUDY

HEBREW
SCRIPTURES
Women in the Bible
FOR
Progressive
Christians

The story of Ruth shows us the pervasiveness of patriarchal structures. Women have no place to turn when they are widowed and fear for their very survival.
– Sharon Pace Jeansonne, *The Storyteller's Companion to the Bible: Vol 4.*

Ruth's speech recognizes that she is switching allegiance, from the family and household and clan of her birth and upbringing to that of Naomi. This is no small thing. Ruth is abandoning all she has known in exchange for a world she does not know. At the same time, she may readily have summed up the situation and realized that neither she nor Naomi have many – if any – prospects, and so figures they have a better chance of survival together than on their own.

In a simple phrase, Naomi acknowledges reality, but also makes a stunning theological point when they arrive back in Bethlehem and are greeted by the people there: "Don't call me Naomi (Pleasant) but call me Mara (Bitter) for *El Shaddai* has made me very bitter." The expression *El Shaddai* is generally translated as "God Almighty," but its roots are ambiguous and, given the strongly female viewpoint of the book, this may come into play. The later meaning of *shad* is mountain; but the earlier one is breast.[5] In the earliest understandings of ancient Hebrew language and culture, God's strength was seen in the ability to provide for the people. It is quite possible, then, that Naomi is thinking of this aspect of God, and that God has failed to feed her and her daughters-in-law. It's a powerful image.

Ruth 2

Now Naomi had a respected relative, a man of worth, through her husband from the family of Elimelech. His name was Boaz. [2] Ruth the Moabite said to Naomi, "Let me go to the field so that I may glean among the ears of grain behind someone in whose eyes I might find favor."

Naomi replied to her, "Go, my daughter." [3] So she went; she arrived and she gleaned in the field behind the harvesters. By chance, it happened to be the portion of the field that belonged to Boaz, who was from the family of Elimelech.

[4] Just then Boaz arrived from Bethlehem. He said to the harvesters, "May the Lord be with you."

And they said to him, "May the Lord bless you."

[5] Boaz said to his young man, the one who was overseeing the harvesters, "To whom does this young woman belong?"

[6] The young man who was overseeing the harvesters

answered, "She's a young Moabite woman, the one who returned with Naomi from the territory of Moab. [7]She said, 'Please let me glean so that I might gather up grain from among the bundles behind the harvesters.' She arrived and has been on her feet from the morning until now, and has sat down for only a moment."

[8]Boaz said to Ruth, "Haven't you understood, my daughter? Don't go glean in another field; don't go anywhere else. Instead, stay here with my young women. [9]Keep your eyes on the field that they are harvesting and go along after them. I've ordered the young men not to assault you. Whenever you are thirsty, go to the jugs and drink from what the young men have filled."

[10]Then she bowed down, face to the ground, and replied to him, "How is it that I've found favor in your eyes, that you notice me? I'm an immigrant." [11]Boaz responded to her, "Everything that you did for your mother-in-law after your husband's death has been reported fully to me: how you left behind your father, your mother, and the land of your birth, and came to a people you hadn't known beforehand. [12]May the Lord reward you for your deed. May you receive a rich reward from the Lord, the God of Israel, under whose wings you've come to seek refuge." [13]She said, "May I continue to find favor in your eyes, sir, because you've comforted me and because you've spoken kindly to your female servant – even though I'm not one of your female servants."

[14]At mealtime Boaz said to her, "Come over here, eat some of the bread, and dip your piece in the vinegar." She sat alongside the harvesters, and he served roasted grain to her. She ate, was satisfied, and had leftovers. [15]Then she got up to glean.

Boaz ordered his young men, "Let her glean between the bundles, and don't humiliate her. [16]Also, pull out some from the bales for her and leave them behind for her to glean. And don't scold her."

[17]So she gleaned in the field until evening. Then she threshed what she had gleaned; it was about an ephah of barley. [18]She picked it up and went into town. Her mother-in-law saw what she had gleaned. She brought out what she had left over after eating her fill and gave it to her. [19]Her mother-in-law said to her, "Where did you glean today? Where did you

work? May the one who noticed you be blessed."

She told her mother-in-law with whom she had worked and said, "The name of the man with whom I worked today is Boaz."

20Naomi replied to her daughter-in-law, "May he be blessed by the Lord, who hasn't abandoned his faithfulness with the living or with the dead." Naomi said to her, "The man is one of our close relatives; he's one of our redeemers [emphasis mine: other translations say "next of kin"].

21Ruth the Moabite replied, "Furthermore, he said to me, 'Stay with my workers until they've finished all of my harvest.'"

22Naomi said to Ruth her daughter-in-law, "It's good, my daughter, that you go out with his young women, so that men don't assault you in another field."

23Thus she stayed with Boaz's young women, gleaning until the completion of the barley and wheat harvests. And she lived with her mother-in-law.

Act two takes place in Bethlehem, and centres around Ruth gleaning in the fields of a man named Boaz. He is a "man of worth" indicating he has both wealth and, probably because of the wealth, power. He is also a relative of Naomi's. Is this mere coincidence? One might think so, but in a biblical story the assumption is always that events are part of God's divine intention.

Gleaning was prescribed by Jewish law and was an important protection that helped the poor to survive. While we may often view ancient Hebrew law as harsh and restrictive, it was in fact quite compassionate for the times, and often made provision for those at the bottom of the social ladder. Gleaning is described in Leviticus 19:9–10 and 23:22. When harvesting, you were not to pick up anything that fell to the ground, nor were you to harvest right to the edge of your property. Rather, whatever fell to the ground and the grain at the edge of your property was to be left for "widows and immigrants" to gather to feed themselves. Deuteronomy 24:19–22 expands this slightly by adding "orphans," and by reminding people that this law exists because they were once slaves themselves (i.e., at the bottom of the ladder) and thus they need to be compassionate toward others. The practice was enshrined in law in various countries over the course of history (notably England and France) and is a common custom in many other parts of the world.

Boaz notices Ruth and asks the overseer who she belongs to. This illustrates the sexism of the time, but within the story it serves to remind us that Ruth does not, in fact, belong to any man – if she "belongs" to anyone, it is to Naomi, to whom she has pledged her allegiance. It may also be a way of saying, "You don't need to belong to a man in order to exist."

Boaz is clearly interested in Ruth despite the fact that she is a Moabite, and he instructs his men not to assault her. As a poor, female foreigner, many young men would simply have seen her as "fair game." Indeed, a woman such as Ruth would have been seen as disposable. But Boaz forbids it. Whether he is being intentional here about pursuing her (which he has the right to do as her deceased husband's relative) or is simply interested in an attractive woman, we cannot know for sure. Whichever is true, he begins the process of redeeming her by declaring, publicly, that she is a person of substance, and not a throwaway slave or a mere foreigner to be overlooked.

When Ruth returns home and tells Naomi what has happened, Naomi is delighted because she knows that Boaz can redeem Ruth (and thus, by extension, Naomi herself). A woman who had been condemned to be one of the living dead now sees a glimmer of hope – and the hand of God behind it all.

Ruth 3

Naomi her mother-in-law said to her, "My daughter, shouldn't I seek security for you, so that things might go well for you? ²Now isn't Boaz, whose young women you were with, our relative? Tonight he will be winnowing barley at the threshing floor. ³You should bathe, put on some perfume, wear nice clothes, and then go down to the threshing floor. Don't make yourself known to the man until he has finished eating and drinking. ⁴When he lies down, notice the place where he is lying. Then go, uncover his feet, and lie down. And he will tell you what to do."

⁵Ruth replied to her, "I'll do everything you are telling me."
⁶So she went down to the threshing floor, and she did everything just as her mother-in-law had ordered.

⁷Boaz ate and drank, and he was in a good mood. He went over to lie down by the edge of the grain pile. Then she quietly approached, uncovered his legs, and lay down. ⁸During the middle of the night, the man shuddered and turned over – and there was a woman lying at his feet. ⁹"Who are you?" he asked.

She replied, "I'm Ruth your servant. Spread out your robe over your servant, because you are a redeemer."

¹⁰He said, "May you be blessed by the Lord, my daughter! You have acted even more faithfully than you did at first. You haven't gone after rich or poor young men. ¹¹And now, my daughter, don't be afraid. I'll do for you everything you are asking. Indeed, my people – all who are at the gate – know that you are a woman of worth. ¹²Now, although it's certainly true that I'm a redeemer, there's a redeemer who is a closer relative than I am. ¹³Stay the night. And in the morning, if he'll redeem you – good, let him redeem. But if he doesn't want to redeem you, then – as the Lord lives – I myself will redeem you. Lie down until the morning."

¹⁴So she lay at his feet until morning. Then she got up before one person could recognize another, for he had said, "No one should know that the woman came to the threshing floor." ¹⁵He said, "Bring the cloak that you have on and hold it out." She held it out, and he measured out six measures of barley and placed it upon her. Then she went into town.

¹⁶She came to her mother-in-law, who said, "How are you, my daughter?"

So Ruth told her everything the man had done for her. ¹⁷She said, "He gave me these six measures of barley, for he said to me, 'Don't go away empty-handed to your mother-in-law.'"

¹⁸"Sit tight, my daughter," Naomi replied, "until you know how it turns out. The man won't rest until he resolves the matter today."

Here in chapter three, the story reaches its apex and the deal is set – even though some of the pieces do not fall into place until the fourth chapter. Naomi plots things out carefully and gives Ruth explicit instructions: bathe, put on perfume, wear nice clothes. In other words, make yourself irresistible.

The instruction to uncover Boaz' feet and lie down (3:4) needs a little unpacking, for it is rife with Hebrew euphemism. To put it bluntly, "feet" is a common euphemism in the Bible for male genitalia, and to "lie down" generally is understood as meaning "to lie down for the purpose of having sex." Putting the two together in this verse leaves little to the imagination: when Boaz has satisfied himself with food and drink, Ruth is to go to him and let nature take its course.

Ruth follows Naomi's instructions and when, in the middle of the night, he awakens and finds Ruth at his "feet" he asks the obvious question: "Who are you?" It's a bit like the scene in some films where someone wakes up in the morning surprised to discover who they went to bed with.

Yet things turn out well. Ruth introduces herself (remember, it would be dark and Boaz is a bit shocked). She asks Boaz to spread his robe over her – a way for a someone to say, "stay the night with me." Boaz is impressed with more than Ruth's beauty and perfume, however, as he remarks on how wonderful and loyal she has been. The fact that he has already thought about the other relative who might have a claim on Ruth, and what he will do if that relative rejects her, indicates that he had already been thinking about how to marry her, so overall the entire event is pleasing. And he invites her to stay.

Ruth wakes up before daylight and prepares to leave, so neither of them is embarrassed or ashamed. Boaz offers Ruth a large amount of barley as a gift, and she goes home. We should hardly be surprised that Naomi is waiting up for her, and Naomi is well pleased – it seems things are turning out just as she had hoped.

Ruth 4

Meanwhile, Boaz went up to the gate and sat down there. Just then, the redeemer about whom Boaz had spoken was passing by. He said, "Sir, come over here and sit down." So he turned aside and sat down. ²Then he took ten men from the town's elders and said, "Sit down here." And they sat down.

³Boaz said to the redeemer, "Naomi, who has returned from the field of Moab, is selling the portion of the field that belonged to our brother Elimelech. ⁴I thought that I should let you know and say, 'Buy it, in the presence of those sitting here and in the presence of the elders of my people.' If you will redeem it, redeem it; but if you won't redeem it, tell me so that I may know. There isn't anyone to redeem it except you, and I'm next in line after you."

He replied, "I will redeem it."

⁵Then Boaz said, "On the day when you buy the field from Naomi, you also buy Ruth the Moabite, the wife of the dead man, in order to preserve the dead man's name for his inheritance."

⁶But the redeemer replied, "Then I can't redeem it for myself, without risking damage to my own inheritance. Redeem it for yourself. You can have my right of redemption, because I'm unable to act as redeemer."

⁷In Israel, in former times, this was the practice regarding redemption and exchange to confirm any such matter: a man would take off his sandal and give it to the other person. This was the process of making a transaction binding in Israel. ⁸Then the redeemer said to Boaz, "Buy it for yourself," and he took off his sandal.

⁹Boaz announced to the elders and all the people, "Today you are witnesses that I've bought from the hand of Naomi all that belonged to Elimelech and all that belonged to Chilion and Mahlon. ¹⁰And also Ruth the Moabite, the wife of Mahlon, I've bought to be my wife, to preserve the dead man's name for his inheritance so that the name of the dead man might not be cut off from his brothers or from the gate of his hometown – today you are witnesses."

¹¹Then all the people who were at the gate and the elders said, "We are witnesses. May the Lord grant that the woman who is coming into your household be like Rachel and like Leah, both of whom built up the house of Israel. May you be fertile in Ephrathah and may you preserve a name in Bethlehem. ¹²And may your household be like the household of Perez, whom Tamar bore to Judah – through the children that the Lord will give you from this young woman."

¹³So Boaz took Ruth, and she became his wife. He was intimate with her, the Lord let her become pregnant, and she gave birth to a son. ¹⁴The women said to Naomi, "May the Lord be blessed, who today hasn't left you without a redeemer. May his name be proclaimed in Israel. ¹⁵He will restore your life and sustain you in your old age. Your daughter-in-law who loves you has given birth to him. She's better for you than seven sons." ¹⁶Naomi took the child and held him to her breast, and she became his guardian. ¹⁷The neighborhood women gave him a name, saying, "A son has been born to Naomi." They called his name Obed.

There is one more bit of business to tend to and Boaz deals with it the next morning. He has already discovered there is another male relative who apparently is more closely related to Elimelech (Naomi's late husband) and thus has "right of first refusal" to perform the ritual of Levirate marriage with Ruth – that is, the right to marry her and have a child with her who will be the descendant of her late husband.

A group of men gather at the town gate to transact the business. Pause and notice for a moment that this bit of business will determine the fate of both Naomi and Ruth, yet neither of them is present nor has any voice in the matter.

Boaz tells the unnamed man that he can buy a piece of land that Naomi is selling. The fact that this male next-of-kin goes unnamed is itself interesting. Usually it's the other way around – the men are named and the women go unnamed. But here, the women are named and this important male character remains anonymous – perhaps another clue that the story was first told by women. The man leaps at the opportunity, but then Boaz casually mentions, "of course you'll also have to marry Naomi's daughter-in-law and any child she has as a result will not be your descendant, and gee, that child will probably inherit the land …" While this is not the way the law was written – or presumably enacted – Boaz has set this situation up so the man will reject the deal, leaving Boaz free to marry Ruth. This explanation of how ancient customs worked is a major clue that the story was written down much later, when people no longer remembered

BIBLE STUDY

HEBREW
SCRIPTURES
Women in the Bible
FOR
Progressive
Christians

the custom – an argument that the story was in fact made up later to support including foreigners in the community.

There is nothing left now but for Boaz and Ruth to marry, and for Ruth to have a child, and all this happens in fairly rapid course.

The focus then shifts to Naomi, who is now fully restored to her humanity, because she has a "son" (technically, a grandson). Beyond that, however, the women point out that this is entirely through the agency of Ruth (not Boaz), who is worth more than seven sons. Seven, being the number of days taken by God to create the world in Genesis 1, is a sacred number implying perfection. Ruth is thus beyond perfection. As a last and wonderful piece, the *women* of the community name the child Obed.

Almost as a footnote to the rest of the book, we are told briefly and without fanfare that Obed had a son named Jesse, who had a son named David. While it's not spelled out clearly, this is a reference to King David. In case there is any doubt, the last four verses of the book provide a genealogy to tell us who some of the male ancestors of David were.

The story is a women's story, however. Yes, the men play highly significant roles and have far more power than anyone should have over others, and they are often the ones making the decisions. Yet were it not for Ruth's astonishing loyalty, Naomi's cunning planning, and Ruth's daring willingness to go along with Naomi's potentially risky plans, the two women would have disappeared into the wilderness, without anyone noticing. As it is, Ruth and Naomi stand as bold symbols of what can be done when we focus not on our own self-interests but on the needs and welfare of others. Beyond that, they remind us that outsiders – even outsiders for whom we may have little respect – can be brave and strong and play a vital role in in society.

Questions

■ Why do you think the stories of Rahab and Ruth were preserved? What might the authors be wanting us to take from them?

■ How are these women similar to – or different from – other women in the Bible?

- What might it mean that the biblical text only mentions casually that Rahab was a prostitute?
- Why do you think Matthew would have included both Rahab and Ruth in the genealogy of Jesus?
- The story of Ruth is probably not factual but was likely offered to help people be more accepting of people of other races, cultures, and clans. How might that fact enhance your reading and understanding of the story?
- How familiar are you with the practice of gleaning? Is it practiced in your community or region today?
- Boaz' assumption that Ruth must belong to a man is met with the simple comment that she is the one who returned with Noami from Moab. To what extent do you think this might be a way of saying that women are not simply the property of men?
- Ruth 2:9 shows us the potential vulnerability of Ruth: her race and stature as a single woman make her vulnerable to sexual exploitation and aggression, after which she could be easily discarded. This brings to mind the ways women are treated around the world, and specifically, in Canada, the issue of Indigenous women who are missing, their cases seldom looked into by the police because they are "only" Indigenous women. Why do you think we tend to see some people – most often women – as disposable? How might we address this?
- The image of a group of men deciding the fate of Naomi and Ruth can be seen as akin to the practices – mercifully falling to the wayside – in our own culture of a man asking a woman's father for permission to marry her, and the custom of a father bringing his daughter to be symbolically "given" to the groom in a marriage ceremony. What has been your response to those aspects of "traditional" marriage ceremonies? How have you noticed them evolve and change over time?
- The story of Ruth was undoubtedly preserved and presented to tell us that we should not just tolerate foreigners in our midst, but actually affirm and embrace them, for they could turn out to be significant in the life of the community. Think of refugees and other "foreigners" who have often been maligned in your community.

BIBLE STUDY

HEBREW SCRIPTURES
Women in the Bible
FOR Progressive Christians

Think, too, of those immigrants and foreigners who have gone on to leave a huge and positive mark on the life of your community. How is God calling us to respond?

■ At the end of the story, the women of the community name the child. While this was normally the mother's activity, it is taken on here by the women as a group. What might this tell us?

■ The rabbis, writing sometime between 200 and 300 CE, grappled with the book of Ruth because Deuteronomy states that no Moabite can become a member of the community for ten generations. The rabbis determined that in the case of Ruth her acceptance by Boaz was okay because the Torah did not say a *Moabitess* could not be welcomed. How does this story challenge us in our understandings of who is to be included in our communities?

SESSION 5

Two Mothers: Hagar and Sarah

We should note that the sweeping stories of the matriarchs and patriarchs of the Judeo-Christian tradition are historically questionable. Extensive archaeological investigation comes up with no evidence of their existence. Does this mean they did not exist? Not at all. But we are invited to question and ponder the stories in a slightly freer way, not one encumbered by facts. These stories are told to explain how the Jewish faith tradition began, and to teach us of God's relations with people in ancient times. Arguing about whether Abraham and Sarah (or any other biblical character) existed or not is to do a fierce disservice to the stories, which are given to us – along with the rest of the Bible – to tell us about God and God's relationship with humankind. They were never presented to prove or disprove anything. It helps, therefore, to read them as stories rather than as factual history, and to let them tell us what they can.

This is important as we approach the story of Hagar, who is a great crossover figure between Judaism and Islam. She appears in both the Bible and the Qur'an, although with different roles in each book. According to the Qur'an she is the first wife of Abraham; an Egyptian woman given to him by Pharaoh during a sojourn to Egypt. According to the Bible, she is Sarah's handmaid, whom she offers to Abraham as a surrogate because Sarah cannot have children. According to both scriptures, Hagar becomes the mother of Ishmael, the ancestor of the Arab peoples. At this point the two stories veer in different directions. The Qur'an tells us that Ishmael is the son chosen by God, whereas the Bible tells us that Hagar and Ishmael are rejected by God, and that Sarah's son, Isaac, is the one through whom all God's promises will be fulfilled. Which version is correct? Obviously, the answer lies in the belief system we carry when we read the stories. Facts to support either story are absent, and that's okay because we are dealing with stories of faith rather than factual events. However, for our purposes here, the key issue is not what happens after, but the stories of the women – Hagar and Sarah – and how the Bible presents them to us.

That Hagar is mentioned positively at all in Jewish scripture is undoubtedly a testament to her strength and ability to find a solution to even the most horrible of conditions. She is a type of surrogate mother and a quintessential single parent, caring for her son Ishmael as both father and mother. She also provides us with an amazing story of someone who dares to stand up against all odds and comes through at the end – if not with a proverbial smile on her face, then at least with a great deal of dignity and strength.

Sarah, on the other hand, is described by Wikipedia as a "biblical matriarch and prophetess, a major figure in Abrahamic religions."[6] Given all she goes through in her life and remembering that prophet/prophetess refers to someone who challenges us to understand the present (and how it can influence the future) the description of "prophetess" is quite well deserved.

We can readily understand Sarah's jealousy of Hagar, given that, according to the story, she spent more than 80 years wanting to have a child of her own. As a person of faith, she is certainly treated as secondary to her husband, Abraham, and we have not been terrifically kind to her by focusing on her laughter and equating it with a lack of faith rather than delight that she is the one God has chosen to bear a child of great importance.

The story of these two women begins with Sarah who, along with Abraham and an entourage of their family, leave Ur (in the land of Chaldea), and relocate to Haran (in the land of Canaan). At this point, they are called Abram and Sarai, but to minimize confusion I will refer to them as Abraham and Sarah. They have the same father but different mothers – not uncommon in those days when men had multiple wives.

The two of them are old. We learn that Abraham is 75 and Sarah is 65– the kind of exaggeration one might expect in any great tale. Also, Hebrew use of numbers was far more fluid than our use of them today, and so the use of these two numbers here is meant to show us they were quite elderly; their exact age is not the issue.

More important than their age, however, is the key wording of Genesis 11:30: "Sarah was unable to have children." This statement invites us to pause and focus, because so much emotion is held in those few words. In any era – but especially during a time when the primary role of women was to bear and raise children – this statement should be understood as telling us that, in the eyes of those in her world, Sarah was less than complete. For Sarah, this is a devastating reality; her infertility will dominate the entire story of Sarah, Hagar, and Abraham.

Let's look at the biblical story in Genesis 12, where we encounter Abraham and Sarah going to Egypt for economic relief during a famine in Canaan.

Genesis 12:10–20

10When a famine struck the land, Abram went down toward Egypt to live as an immigrant since the famine was so severe in the land. 11Just before he arrived in Egypt, he said to his wife Sarai, "I know you are a good-looking woman. 12When the Egyptians see you, they will say, 'This is his wife,' and they will kill me but let you live. 13So tell them you are my sister so that they will treat me well for your sake, and I will survive because of you."

14When Abram entered Egypt, the Egyptians saw how beautiful his wife was. 15When Pharaoh's princes saw her, they praised her to Pharaoh; and the woman was taken into Pharaoh's household. 16Things went well for Abram because of her: he acquired flocks, cattle, male donkeys, men servants, women servants, female donkeys, and camels. 17Then the Lord struck Pharaoh and his household with severe plagues because of Abram's wife Sarai. 18So Pharaoh summoned Abram and said, "What's this you've done to me? Why didn't you tell me she was your wife? 19Why did you say, 'She's my sister,' so that I made her my wife? Now, here's your wife. Take her and go!" 20Pharaoh gave his men orders concerning Abram, and they expelled him with his wife and everything he had.

Abraham and Sarah go to Egypt because they need food and Abraham tells his wife that she will be introduced only as his sister. This, it should be noted, is to save Abraham's life, but puts Sarah at risk. Granted, we are told that this is all because Sarah is irresistibly beautiful, but her opinion is not considered. She is taken into Pharaoh's household and later (12:19) we are told that Pharaoh made her his wife, meaning he had sex with her. This invites us to question if she truly was 65, as the suggestion of her attractiveness and sexual desirability would imply she was younger.

The ancient rabbis believed that Sarah cried out to God, complaining that Abraham benefitted handsomely from this arrangement while she suffered greatly, even noting she was "imprisoned in Pharaoh's harem." Sarah has been trafficked as a plaything so that things go well for Abraham ; this is not a pleasant story.

Genesis 16:1–16

Sarai, Abram's wife, had not been able to have children. Since she had an Egyptian servant named Hagar, ²Sarai said to Abram, "The Lord has kept me from giving birth, so go to my servant. Maybe she will provide me with children." Abram did just as Sarai said. ³After Abram had lived ten years in the land of Canaan, Abram's wife Sarai took her Egyptian servant Hagar and gave her to her husband Abram as his wife. ⁴He slept with Hagar, and she became pregnant. But when she realized that she was pregnant, she no longer respected her mistress. ⁵Sarai said to Abram, "This harassment is your fault. I allowed you to embrace my servant, but when she realized she was pregnant, I lost her respect. Let the Lord decide who is right, you or me."

⁶Abram said to Sarai, "Since she's your servant, do whatever you wish to her." So Sarai treated her harshly, and she ran away from Sarai.

⁷The Lord's messenger found Hagar at a spring in the desert, the spring on the road to Shur, ⁸and said, "Hagar! Sarai's servant! Where did you come from and where are you going?"

She said, "From Sarai my mistress. I'm running away."

⁹The Lord's messenger said to her, "Go back to your mistress. Put up with her harsh treatment of you." ¹⁰The Lord's messenger also said to her,

*"I will give you many children,
        so many they can't be counted!"*
*¹¹The Lord's messenger said to her,
"You are now pregnant and will give birth to a son.
    You will name him Ishmael
    because the Lord has heard about your harsh treatment.
¹²He will be a wild mule of a man;
    he will fight everyone, and they will fight him.
    He will live at odds with all his relatives."
    ¹³Hagar named the Lord who spoke to her, "You are El Roi" because she said, "Can I still see after he saw me?" ¹⁴Therefore, that well is called Beer-lahai-roi; it's the well between Kadesh and Bered. ¹⁵Hagar gave birth to a son for Abram, and Abram named him Ishmael. ¹⁶Abram was 86 years old when Hagar gave birth to Ishmael for Abram.*

We are reminded again that Sarah cannot have children and so she suggests that Abraham have sex with her servant Hagar in the hopes of having the child Abraham so anxiously desires, and which God has promised. Some people struggle with this and want to see it as an adulterous arrangement, but in biblical times it was not at all uncommon. Children were considered so vital to the structure of society and simply for survival that arrangements were allowed to ensure that they were conceived. Because Sarah is Abraham's wife, she is legally the mother of Ishmael, but the fact that Hagar remains as the active mother causes tension. Emotions alone come to the forefront, and we can easily image Sarah questioning her self-worth and value as a result of her inability to have children.

Hagar plays a role here similar to surrogacy in modern Western society, although with two notable exceptions: 1) she has no say in the matter, and 2) she clearly remains a vital part of her child's life, even if legally she is not its mother. That said, increasingly in our modern world, children born in surrogate and even via sperm donor arrangements have varying kinds of ongoing relationship with the parent who is not raising them; in this regard, our ideas about parenthood are ever-changing.

Another piece we cannot truly know is whether Sarah really wants to go through with this. The way the story evolves suggests it is not really her desire but may be her "idea" only because she can see no other solution. Offering Hagar must remind Sarah of her inability to provide her husband with the one thing he desires the most, and certainly serves to strengthen Sarah's feelings of inadequacy and failure.

Trouble swells up when Hagar becomes pregnant. Sarah feels Hagar is looking down on her, taking on an air of "I'm better than you" because she has become pregnant when Sarah was not able to. This may indeed be how Hagar behaved, or could be more Sarah's sense of unworthiness that has caused her to feel this way. She wants rid of Hagar and, while she seems to forget that this was her idea in the first place, she asks Abraham to deal with Hagar. Abraham is presumably torn and passes the responsibility for making a decision back to Sarah.

Sarah treats Hagar harshly and Hagar runs away. While this takes us back to square one, it solves the problem of the conflict between Sarah and Hagar. In a standard television show, Hagar would be banished, the scene would fade, there would be a commercial break, and then Hagar would be gone from the show. But in this story, the author has God intervene. God's messenger (translated "angel" in some versions) finds Hagar and has a conversation with her. The messenger intervenes to the point of sending her back home.

Verse 13 appears differently in early versions of the Genesis manuscripts, which suggests some "correction" of the text took place at some point, but which leaves us wondering a bit about how to translate it. The *Common English Bible*, above, renders verse 13 as "Hagar named the Lord who spoke to her, 'You are El Roi' because she said, 'Can I still see after he saw me?'" but *The Voice* renders it as "I'm going to call you 'God of Seeing' because in this place I have seen the One who watches over me."

Genesis 21:8–21

⁸*The boy [Isaac] grew and stopped nursing. On the day he stopped nursing, Abraham prepared a huge banquet.* ⁹*Sarah saw Hagar's son laughing, the one Hagar the Egyptian had*

borne to Abraham. ¹⁰So she said to Abraham, "Send this servant away with her son! This servant's son won't share the inheritance with my son Isaac."

¹¹This upset Abraham terribly because the boy was his son. ¹²God said to Abraham, "Don't be upset about the boy and your servant. Do everything Sarah tells you to do because your descendants will be traced through Isaac. ¹³But I will make of your servant's son a great nation too, because he is also your descendant." ¹⁴Abraham got up early in the morning, took some bread and a flask of water, and gave it to Hagar. He put the boy in her shoulder sling and sent her away.

She left and wandered through the desert near Beer-sheba. ¹⁵Finally the water in the flask ran out, and she put the boy down under one of the desert shrubs. ¹⁶She walked away from him about as far as a bow shot and sat down, telling herself, I can't bear to see the boy die. She sat at a distance, cried out in grief, and wept.

¹⁷God heard the boy's cries, and God's messenger called to Hagar from heaven and said to her, "Hagar! What's wrong? Don't be afraid. God has heard the boy's cries over there. ¹⁸Get up, pick up the boy, and take him by the hand because I will make of him a great nation." ¹⁹Then God opened her eyes, and she saw a well. She went over, filled the water flask, and gave the boy a drink. ²⁰God remained with the boy; he grew up, lived in the desert, and became an expert archer. ²¹He lived in the Paran desert, and his mother found him an Egyptian wife.

For readers of the Bible who understand that Isaac becomes the favoured child, there is no element of surprise that the "other" son, Ishmael, must be sent away. What is somewhat surprising, however, is how the author treats Hagar in this story – especially given that in the Qur'an Sarah is *not* portrayed as treating Hagar with hostility. Does it suggest, for example, that at the time of writing the authors of the Qur'an felt more generously towards or held more respect for the Hebraic tradition, or for Sarah at least, than the Hebrew writers did for their Arabic neighbours or cousins?

That said and leaving aside for a moment the fact that the authors and compilers of each holy book (the Bible and the Qur'an) intended to support their own cultural dynasty through their respective foundational stories (Hagar/Ishmael and Sarah/Isaac), there is also the reality that in any story that focuses on one woman or character more than another, the author will pay more attention to that character's feelings and responses.

Verses 8-10 suggest that Hagar is a nobody, or at least a figure who is simply in the way. The key is the disposal of Ishmael, and Hagar needs to be banished with him. Sarah is jealous that Ishmael is playing with Isaac, which seems innocuous enough. However, we can readily see that the deeper jealousy comes from the fact that Sarah is worried that Abraham will end up preferring Ishmael, and/or Hagar. Thus, Sarah believes they must be sent away, and says so.

Abraham is distressed. She is portrayed here as the stronger one in that marriage, and in this instance, God is depicted as supporting her choice.

In reality, if this was a historical account of an actual situation, given the authority men had over their wives it is likely that Abraham would simply have said, "No! Ishmael is my son, and Hagar is your servant, and I say they can stay." It begs the question, *what was the author thinking?*

God assures Abraham that Isaac is the one through whom the promise will be fulfilled, but that Ishmael will also become a great nation, on account of him being Abraham's son. Hagar and Ishmael are sent away. Soon thirst (and presumably hunger) take over. Hagar sets her child down and goes away from him to a place by herself, uttering the tragic words, "Don't let me see my child die!" This part of the story is honoured in Islam through one of the rituals of the Hajj – the pilgrimage that Muslims are to perform at least once in their lifetime. People run between two hills as a way of replicating Hagar running in search of food and water for her child. This ritual is done to honour motherhood.

Hagar cries in despair, yet we are told that God hears not her cries but those of Ishmael. Is this simply an error – did the original story suggest that God heard *her* cries? It is certainly possible, although God's messenger then affirms that God has heard *the child's* cries. Some have seen in this part of the story a belief that God responds to the cries of a male rather than a female, which could fit with the sexist understandings of the times. But we should tread lightly here. The author may have wanted people to understand that God hears the cries of those with the least power – and that would be a child rather than an adult. Given that God's messenger speaks freely to Hagar, this is probably more believable than any kind of sexism in the text. One can find lots of sexism in the Bible, but we need to be careful not to insert it when it is unwarranted. Hagar is not in any way unimportant in this story – rather, it is Ishmael's vulnerability as a child that causes his voice to be heard, not his status as a male.

A few final things to note. Genesis 21:20 tells us that God is with Ishmael throughout his time of growing up, suggesting that he has not in any way been abandoned. Second, and most importantly for completing the story of Hagar, this same verse tells us that she finds Ishmael a wife in Egypt. This task normally fell to the father; the fact that Hagar does it underscores the fact that she is a single parent, taking on the roles of both mother and father.

Hagar's story ends here, and Sarah's continues. Hagar reminds us that God cares about the vulnerable, those who might at first glance seem obscure or not worthy of our notice. She stands proudly as one who tries to make the best of a situation that none would envy and seeks the best for her child throughout his life. For this, God blesses her child – arguably the best reward any parent could desire.

Genesis 17:15–22

¹⁵*God said to Abraham, "As for your wife Sarai, you will no longer call her Sarai. Her name will now be Sarah.* ¹⁶*I will bless her and even give you a son from her. I will bless her so that she will become nations, and kings of peoples will come from her."*

¹⁷*Abraham fell on his face and laughed. He said to himself, Can a 100-year-old man become a father, or Sarah, a 90-year-old woman, have a child?* ¹⁸*To God Abraham said, "If only you would accept Ishmael!"*

¹⁹*But God said, "No, your wife Sarah will give birth to a son for you, and you will name him Isaac. I will set up my*

covenant with him and with his descendants after him as an enduring covenant. [20]As for Ishmael, I've heard your request. I will bless him and make him fertile and give him many, many descendants. He will be the ancestor of twelve tribal leaders, and I will make a great nation of him. [21]But I will set up my covenant with Isaac, who will be born to Sarah at this time next year." [22]When God finished speaking to him, God ascended, leaving Abraham alone.

God tells Abraham that he and Sarah are now to have new names. According to Rabbi Adam Morris, writing in *Seasons of the Spirit*, the change involves adding the Hebrew letter *hay* to their names. This is one of the letters in God's name, *Yahweh*. Adding it to their names is akin to labelling them as "new and improved," and celebrates the presence of God in their lives. Morris adds that "it is definitely a lot less silly-looking than pasting in big, colourful letters the words 'NEW and IMPROVED' on their foreheads!"[7]

God then tells Abraham that Sarah will have a child. What is Abraham's response? He falls on his face and laughs. So often this part of the story is forgotten, or missed – I have in fact frequently had people (including more than one member of the clergy) challenge me when I have said this. We want to see the laughter of Sarah later in the story as a demonstration of her lack of faith, and thus we struggle when Abraham does the same thing first.

Note also that Abraham and Sarah are much older here. The author wants us to realize that they have aged and that the chances of Sarah having a child have gone from impossible to laughable – literally. They are to have a child, God proclaims, and the child is to be named Isaac, which is Hebrew for laughter.

Genesis 18:1–15

The Lord appeared to Abraham at the oaks of Mamre while he sat at the entrance of his tent in the day's heat. [2]He looked up and suddenly saw three men standing near him. As soon as he saw them, he ran from his tent entrance to greet them and bowed deeply. [3]He said, "Sirs, if you would be so kind, don't just pass by your servant. [4]Let a little water be brought so you may wash your feet and refresh yourselves under the tree. [5]Let me offer you a little bread so you will feel stronger, and after that you may leave your servant and go on your way – since you have visited your servant."

They responded, "Fine. Do just as you have said."

⁶So Abraham hurried to Sarah at his tent and said, "Hurry! Knead three [measures] of the finest flour and make some baked goods!" ⁷Abraham ran to the cattle, took a healthy young calf, and gave it to a young servant, who prepared it quickly. ⁸Then Abraham took butter, milk, and the calf that had been prepared, put the food in front of them, and stood under the tree near them as they ate.

⁹They said to him, "Where's your wife Sarah?"

And he said, "Right here in the tent."

¹⁰Then one of the men said, "I will definitely return to you about this time next year. Then your wife Sarah will have a son!"

Sarah was listening at the tent door behind him. ¹¹Now Abraham and Sarah were both very old. Sarah was no longer menstruating. ¹²So Sarah laughed to herself, thinking, I'm no longer able to have children and my husband's old.

¹³The Lord said to Abraham, "Why did Sarah laugh and say, 'Me give birth? At my age?' ¹⁴Is anything too difficult for the Lord? When I return to you about this time next year, Sarah will have a son."

¹⁵Sarah lied and said, "I didn't laugh," because she was frightened.

But he said, "No, you laughed."

This is clearly the pivotal part of Sarah's story – and, frankly, of Abraham's as well– even though his story is much longer and filled with many other aspects. The birth of a child – especially a son – meant virtually everything in those times. Having a child would ensure that there was someone bound by law and tradition to care for you when you grew old and could not take care of yourself, and who would also guarantee that you would be remembered. If you didn't or couldn't have a child – and more specifically a son – people assumed it was because God was angry with you, even if the reason was unknown. Accordingly, this story about Abraham and Sarah learning they would have a son is key to knowing their

BIBLE STUDY

HEBREW
SCRIPTURES
Women in the Bible
FOR
Progressive
Christians

lives and memories would continue, and that God was pleased with them.

A clear feature of this story is that the promise to Abraham can only be brought to fullest flower through Sarah. She is more important at this point in the story than her husband, because *she* is the one to have a child. Of course, when she hears the promise, she has (understandably) difficulty believing it. Her observation is telling: she believes she cannot have a child because she is "no longer" able, and because her husband is too old. Some have interpreted this to mean that she might have been pregnant previously (perhaps several times) and had miscarried.

The visitors (we assume they are "angels" – everyday-looking people who bring messages from God) have conversation about Sarah's laughter. We often leap to the conclusion they are angry, and that she should not have done it. But perhaps that's not the case. Perhaps they simply want to push the obvious: "Why did you laugh? I mean, you're 90 years old but other than that, why not believe it?!" Sarah denies laughing, and is reminded – again, quite possibly very gently – that she did. This could be seen as scolding but could also just as easily be seen as gentle chiding and may carry the assurance that it's okay to laugh at ludicrous suggestions. The exchange does not have to be taken as meaning they are angry for her apparent lack of faith. Because Sarah is not punished for this behaviour, we should assume that the author was not trying to create a scenario for the purpose of showing God's anger. It is also worth pointing out that Sarah may be among the first to question God in the scriptures, but she is far from the last.

Genesis 21:1–7

The Lord was attentive to Sarah just as he had said, and the Lord carried out just what he had promised her. ²She became pregnant and gave birth to a son for Abraham when he was old, at the very time God had told him. ³Abraham named his son – the one Sarah bore him – Isaac. ⁴Abraham circumcised his son Isaac when he was eight days old just as God had commanded him. ⁵Abraham was 100 years old when his son Isaac was born. ⁶Sarah said, "God has given me laughter. Everyone who hears about it will laugh with me." ⁷She said, "Who could have told Abraham that Sarah would nurse sons? But now I've given birth to a son when he was old!"

Sarah becomes pregnant and has a child. Abraham names him Isaac – laughter – in light presumably of his own laughter as well as that of Sarah. We might understand the name in the sense of "Delight" or "Great Joy," which would be logical names for a child born at such a late stage of life. (I knew a couple who actually named their first and only child – born when both parents were in their mid-40s – Isaac Surprise!)

Sarah's response to the child's name is intriguing. The generally accepted translation is "She said, 'Who could have told Abraham that Sarah would nurse sons? But now I've given birth to a son when he was old!'" However, there is an alternative rendering: "God has made a joke of me. Everyone who hears about it will laugh at me." Given the principle that translators use, that generally no one would alter an ancient manuscript to make it more difficult – we are left to wonder if this was the original that was later changed. If that is indeed the case, is it not telling that Sarah continues to find humour – albeit somewhat dark humour – in the birth of a child in her old age. Some traditions have seen the name Isaac not as "laughter" but rather as "joke," and that may be suggested by this rendering of 21:7.

Genesis 23:1–2

Sarah lived to be 127 years old; this was how long she lived. ²She died in Kiriath-arba, that is, in Hebron, in the land of Canaan; and Abraham cried out in grief and wept for Sarah.

The story of Sarah ends, and the story of Isaac and his descendants will take centre stage. If, in the story, Sarah gave birth at the age of 90 and dies at 127, the author wants us to know that she witnessed a large portion of Isaac's life. This was considered a great bonus; having the child was gift enough and getting to raise the child was an even greater gift from God.

Given everything the couple has endured in their long life – relocation, famine, more travelling, conflict with Hagar and Ishmael, yearning for a child of their own – it is no surprise that Abraham is overcome with major grief at the death of Sarah.

***

We are left, then, with this amazing story of two women, both of whom defy overwhelming odds. The fact that neither woman is treated well and that both are invariably seen as secondary to Abraham, the central male character, is not surprising given the era in which the story in Genesis was written down. Does this mean their stories excuse, or can be used as an excuse for patriarchal culture? I don't think so, for the mere presence of these women in this story is astonishing in itself, and is the message that, through them, we can understand how God's promises can come to fruition, no matter what. Not bad. Not bad at all.

Questions

■ How are Sarah and Hagar similar to – or different from – other biblical women?

■ What are the take-aways for us from their stories?

■ As you read the verse "Sarai was unable to have children," what feelings arise for you? How do you think Sarah responded to that reality in her own life?

■ No mention is made in the story of Hagar's feelings, though these are implied in the fact that she ran away from Sarah. What words would you use to fill the spaces or silences in the text?

■ That the entire story of these two women is told completely from a dominant male perspective is astonishingly clear in Genesis 12:16, where we are told that "things went well for Abraham because of Sarah." No mention is made of her own feelings. Think of situations with which you are familiar where a man benefits from the presence or actions of a woman who has no say in the matter. What feelings arise for you? How might we change this?

- Reflecting on the story of Sarah being imprisoned in Pharaoh's harem, ancient rabbis noted that God responded by telling Sarah that this was all being done for her safety, too, and that her great sacrifice would always be remembered. Has this part of the story really been remembered? In your mind, does that address her suffering?
- Traditional Judaism has assumed that Sarah slept with the Egyptian pharaoh, yet Christianity has generally assumed she did not. Why do you think there is this difference (bearing in mind that the story probably is not factual)?
- Some people have expressed concern about surrogate parenting today, seeing it as going against God's designs for humanity. Yet as we see here and in other biblical stories, surrogate parenting was practiced in ancient times. What are the pros and cons of surrogacy – either the way it was practiced then (sexually) or now (clinically)?
- Abraham does not want to intervene between Sarah and Hagar but gives Sarah permission to do whatever she wants to Hagar. What do you think of Abraham's stance here? How else might he have responded? How might things have turned out if he had acted differently?
- Verse 4 states that Hagar no longer respected her mistress once she learned she was pregnant. This is hardly surprising, seeing as she was able to achieve what Sarah could not. Imagine the relationship and feelings the two women were experiencing. What would it be like to be Hagar? What would it be like to be Sarah? How might you resolve this dilemma?
- Abraham laughs when he learns that Sarah is to have a child. Many of us do not know this, especially given that this story is not included in the *Revised Common Lectionary*, while the story of Sarah's laughter is. Why might this be? How might those in authority be trying to skew our understanding of this story?
- The possibility is presented in chapter 18 that Sarah may have been pregnant before and might have miscarried. What element would this add to the overall story?

BIBLE STUDY

HEBREW SCRIPTURES
Women in the Bible
FOR
Progressive Christians

- Sarah's laughter may be seen by the visitors – and thus by us – as gentle chiding rather than scolding. It may be a reminder that laughing at what appear to be strange suggestions from God is okay. How do you feel about this idea?

- An alternate translation of Genesis 12:7 is "God has made a joke of me; everyone who hears about this will laugh at me." What do you think of this translation? Does it make more or less sense to you? Why do you think translators have chosen the words they did?

SESSION 6

The Women of the Exodus: Puah, Shiphrah, and Miriam

Like the stories of Abraha m, Sarah, and Hagar, the stories found in Exodus are seen by some scholars as fiction since there is no archeological or textual evidence to support them beyond the stories themselves. Yet not all scholars agree. Richard Elliott Friedman is one who argues, convincingly, that a much smaller group of Jews probably left Egypt, and that the stories in Exodus are understandable exaggerations.[8] In similar fashion, scholar Carol Meyers argues that there's another way to look at the question of whether these stories happened or not; it's not necessarily a matter of fact or fiction, yes or no.

> *There's something called mnemohistory, or memory history, that I find particularly useful in thinking about biblical materials. It's not like the history that individuals may have of their own families, which tends to survive only a generation or two. Rather, it's a kind of collective cultural memory.*
>
> *When a group of people experience things that are extremely important to their existence as a group, they often maintain collective memories of these events over generations. And these memories are probably augmented and elaborated and maybe even ritualized as a way of maintaining their relevance ...*
>
> *The Moses of the Bible is larger than life. [He's] a diplomat negotiating with the pharaoh ... a lawgiver bringing the Ten Commandments, the Covenant, down from Sinai ... a military man leading the Israelites in battles ... [he] organizes Israel's judiciary ... and [is] a quasi-priestly figure involved in offering sacrifices and setting up the priestly complex, the tabernacle ... And, of course, he's also a person, a family man.*
>
> *Now, no one individual could possibly have done all that. So the tales are a kind of aggrandizement ...*[9]

BIBLE STUDY

HEBREW
SCRIPTURES
Women in the Bible
FOR
Progressive Christians

It's helpful to keep all of this in mind as we look at the women in these stories.

The book of Exodus begins, of course, with a powerful tale about how the infant Moses survives a number of seemingly insurmountable odds only with the assistance of various women; it is *their* ingenuity and quick action that give him life. While Moses has come to be seen as the most important leader in Jewish history and is credited with giving the law and leading the people into freedom, he would never have managed any of it had it not been for the women who conspired, with God, to keep him alive. These women are crucial to the story of the great hero of the nation. This cannot be overlooked as we explore the story presented in Exodus 1:8 – 2:10.

Exodus 1:8 – 2:10

[8]Now a new king came to power in Egypt who didn't know Joseph. [9]He said to his people, "The Israelite people are now larger in number and stronger than we are. [10]Come on, let's be smart and deal with them. Otherwise, they will only grow in number. And if war breaks out, they will join our enemies, fight against us, and then escape from the land." [11]As a result, the Egyptians put foremen of forced work gangs over the Israelites to harass them with hard work. They had to build storage cities named Pithom and Rameses for Pharaoh. [12]But the more they were oppressed, the more they grew and spread, so much so that the Egyptians started to look at the Israelites with disgust and dread. [13]So the Egyptians enslaved the Israelites. [14]They made their lives miserable with hard labor, making mortar and bricks, doing field work, and by forcing them to do all kinds of other cruel work.

[15]The king of Egypt spoke to two Hebrew midwives named Shiphrah and Puah: [16]"When you are helping the Hebrew women give birth and you see the baby being born, if it's a boy, kill him. But if it's a girl, you can let her live." [17]Now the two midwives respected God so they didn't obey the Egyptian king's order. Instead, they let the baby boys live.

[18] So the king of Egypt called the two midwives and said to them, "Why are you doing this? Why are you letting the baby boys live?"

> [19] The two midwives said to Pharaoh, "Because Hebrew women aren't like Egyptian women. They're much stronger and give birth before any midwives can get to them." [20] So God treated the midwives well, and the people kept on multiplying and became very strong. [21] And because the midwives respected God, God gave them households of their own.
>
> [22] Then Pharaoh gave an order to all his people: "Throw every baby boy born to the Hebrews into the Nile River, but you can let all the girls live."
>
> [2:1] Now a man from Levi's household married a Levite woman. [2] The woman became pregnant and gave birth to a son. She saw that the baby was healthy and beautiful, so she hid him for three months. [3] When she couldn't hide him any longer, she took a reed basket and sealed it up with black tar. She put the child in the basket and set the basket among the reeds at the riverbank. [4] The baby's older sister stood watch nearby to see what would happen to him.
>
> [5] Pharaoh's daughter came down to bathe in the river, while her women servants walked along beside the river. She saw the basket among the reeds, and she sent one of her servants to bring it to her. [6] When she opened it, she saw the child. The boy was crying, and she felt sorry for him. She said, "This must be one of the Hebrews' children."
>
> [7] Then the baby's sister said to Pharaoh's daughter, "Would you like me to go and find one of the Hebrew women to nurse the child for you?"
>
> [8] Pharaoh's daughter agreed, "Yes, do that." So the girl went and called the child's mother. [9] Pharaoh's daughter said to her, "Take this child and nurse it for me, and I'll pay you for your work." So the woman took the child and nursed it. [10] After the child had grown up, she brought him back to Pharaoh's daughter, who adopted him as her son. She named him Moses, "because," she said, "I pulled him out of the water."

The story of the exodus is without any question the most significant biblical story for the Jewish faith. A key part of that story, in turn, is the presence of Moses and the leadership he provides to the Jewish people. Yet the roles of his sister Miriam and brother Aaron should not be overlooked. Aaron becomes his brother's spokesperson appointed by God at the burning bush when Moses declares that he cannot speak well. Miriam plays a key role when the people arrive at last on the non-Egyptian side of the water. She is also instrumental in the story of the infant Moses' survival.

It has been said that the lengthy story of Joseph and his brothers was told primarily as a device to show why or how the people of Israel ended up in Egypt in the first place. This is of course debatable, but it suggests how vital the story is. In similar fashion, before Moses can have an encounter with God, a confrontation with Pharaoh, and then ultimately lead the people into freedom, he needs to be born. And that's a key story that would not happen without a brilliant sequence of events orchestrated by women.

Juxtaposed against these women is a rather stupid Egyptian pharaoh, or king. The ancient rabbis said that any shrewd king would have set out not to kill the male children, but the females, seeing as "it is the women who give birth to and nurture any nation."[10] Similarly, Pharaoh appears to set tasks for the Hebrews that are impossible to fulfill; ancient Egyptian records indicate the Jewish men were required to produce 2,000 or even 3,000 bricks each per day, an incomprehensible amount.[11] Should they fail, they would be beaten, which would then render them even less fit to produce a large number the next day. Not a great way for even a dictator to run a business!

The first women we encounter in this story are the two midwives, Shiphrah and Puah. It is interesting that they are named, even though the pharaoh is not; some historians believe it was Rameses II, but this is not certain. In any event, these two women who do totally female-centric work are given names. This must not be overlooked; they are truly the heroes of the story. Pharaoh summons them and commands them to kill any boy that the Hebrew women birth.

The two women leave and promptly agree to disobey the king's order, choosing instead to obey God. Legends suggest that they not only allowed the boys to live but helped hide them and helped obtain food and supplies for them so they would grow and be strong.

The furious king summons the midwives to ask them what's

going on, and they give an almost ludicrous answer: "Why," they say, "those Hebrew women have their babies so fast by the time we get to them they're all done." As further evidence of how stupid the king is, he falls for this.

By way of rewarding them for their faithfulness, God gives the midwives households of their own, which was quite unheard of. This again elevates them to a much higher status than they might ordinarily have had. In a story about the birth of a great male leader, these two women are truly the key players.

The king then follows up with a new order: throw all the baby boys into the Nile River.

In chapter two, the scene narrows to the birth of a specific child, Moses, although he will not be named until the end of the story. His mother (Jochebed, according to Exodus 6:20, although again not named here) found him to be "healthy and beautiful" and so she hid him for three months. When she can no longer hide him, she decides to put him in a basket and place him in the river. In doing this, she is theoretically obeying the king's order (casting her baby boy into the Nile) but she does it in a way that she hopes will enable him somehow to survive. Of course, putting a helpless infant in a basket at the edge of a river, especially one known for being infested with crocodiles is several steps beyond risky. However, it is a great addition to the story, and, beyond that, it shows Jochebed's fierce determination to protect her child from immediate death at the hands of the authorities. We are reminded of some of the amazing and fearless acts mothers, fathers, and strangers performed to protect children during the Holocaust.

While we tend to translate the Hebrew word *tevah* as basket, especially within the context of this story, it is an intriguing word. Its only other appearance in the Bible is when it is used to refer to the vessel that Noah builds, an ark to protect creation from God's wrath. Interesting, then, that this is the word used here. It is undoubtedly no accident, and the translation "basket" rather lessens the powerful strength of the Hebrew word.

Another woman enters the scene here, the baby's older sister. She is also unnamed at this point in the story, but we can safely assume that this refers to Miriam, the older sister of Moses that we shall meet later in the book of Exodus. She watches to see what happens to the baby. This is not the safest or easiest of tasks for a child, which again heightens the power of women in the story – Miriam is just a young girl, yet she watches Moses to ensure his safety and survival.

Pharaoh's daughter – Egyptian records tell us that Rameses II had 59 daughters! – comes to bathe at the river. The ancient rabbis believed that she had leprosy (a generic term for any kind of skin disease in biblical times) and that explains why she is not named, and why she needed to bathe in the river as opposed to at the palace.[12] We have no way of knowing if this is true, but it would place her as yet another outsider in the story, for anyone with leprosy (even a princess) was generally banned from participating in everyday society. This was the case across a wide range of cultures. She also would not have been allowed to marry, which might explain her eagerness to "adopt" a foreign child. It certainly adds an intriguing element to the story.

When the princess picks up the child, the sister (Miriam) steps forward and offers to find a Hebrew woman who can nurse and care for the child. Thinking this a great offer, the princess agrees and thus Jochebed is paid to raise her own son.

Some have wondered how Miriam and the princess could communicate, assuming that one spoke Egyptian and the other Hebrew. However, given that the Jews have been living in Egypt for centuries it is not at all surprising that Miriam would speak Egyptian – at the very least enough to get by in a simple conversation. Oppressed and enslaved peoples are generally forced to abandon their own languages in favour of the oppressor's language (think of African slaves in the U.S., Indigenous children in residential schools in Canada and Australia, or Blacks during the apartheid regime in South Africa).

At the end of this section, we learn that when Moses had "grown up" – we aren't told how old he was – Jochebed took him to the palace where the princess adopted him and raised him. Moses will do a number of great things, but let us stay with the story of

Miriam, who goes on to play a significant role later in the book of Exodus, as the people cross the Sea of Reeds.

Given that most people are familiar with the Exodus story, I'll offer only the briefest of summaries. Moses gets angry when he sees an Egyptian slave master beat a Hebrew slave. In his rage, he kills the master. He then flees to the wilderness, to avoid nasty consequences, where one day he encounters God in a burning bush. God speaks to Moses about how difficult it has been to see how the Egyptians treat the Hebrews (Moses can relate) and so God has decided to rescue them. Moses is to lead them. When Moses balks, God answers his protests and tells Moses that his brother, Aaron, can speak on his behalf if he gets cold feet. Moses confronts Pharaoh who, despite being smitten by numerous plagues from God, does not let them leave. Finally, Pharaoh relents, only to change his mind and order the Egyptian army to follow and slaughter them. When the Jews arrive at the Sea of Reeds, they believe they are trapped, but God intervenes to make the waters recede and they cross just in time for the waters to rush back and destroy the Egyptian army.

Exodus 15 begins by telling us that Moses and all the people then sang a song. At that point, we encounter Miriam once more. The passage is a mere two verses – compared to the 18 verses that made up the song Moses sang with the people – but these two verses are potent and intriguing.

Exodus 15:20–21

²⁰Then the prophet Miriam, Aaron's sister, took a tambourine in her hand. All the women followed her playing tambourines and dancing. ²¹Miriam sang the refrain back to them:
Sing to the Lord, for an overflowing victory!
Horse and rider he threw into the sea!

Miriam is called a prophet. Let us not miss this, for the word is frequently and lavishly bestowed on men but not so often on women. Miriam is in fact the first woman to bear this title in the Bible. Remember that a biblical prophet is not someone who foretells the future, but rather someone who speaks honestly about the current realities in which we find ourselves, sometimes making predictions about what will follow if we do not change our ways. Accordingly, the act of grabbing a tambourine and spontaneously leading the women in a vibrant dance is most intriguing.

The brief song is in sharp contrast to that of Moses in Exodus 15:1–18, where God's destruction of the Egyptian army is described in detail. Miriam's song merely praises God for an overwhelming victory, having thrown the horse and rider into the sea. While Moses' song celebrates God the mighty (male) warrior, who defeats the enemy as if a battle had raged, Miriam's song simply notes the miraculous intervention of the tides – presumably at God's arrangement. Beyond that, numerous unnamed women immediately join Miriam in her song, dancing and making music with their tambourines. What possessed these women, who had to rapidly pack for a hasty flight from Egypt, to also bring musical instruments? We can only assume that even in the face of threat and danger they had enough faith to know that God would give them a reason to sing and dance with joy and praise once again. This is such a great gift, a reminder that in the midst of the most anxious and frightening of moments we can know that God is with us.

The stories of Miriam and Moses continue, but for our purposes we stop here. In reflecting on the story, we must name the women again: Shiphrah, Puah, Jochebed, Miriam, and the princess. Each of these women is a powerful hero who risks a great deal in order to further what is clearly presented in the story as God's plan. Without the intervention of each of them, Moses would presumably never have survived. God moves and acts in mysterious and wondrous ways, and we are invited to marvel and give thanks. In the book of Exodus women give life, women sustain life, and women celebrate God's miraculous presence in the midst of daily life. We must ensure that these pieces do not get lost or buried in the other biblical stories, for they are pivotal.

Questions

- Why do you think the author included all these women in this part of the story of Moses?
- How are they similar to – or different from – other biblical women?
- While history has shown some fierce female leaders, their policies and actions have often been greatly influenced by the men around them. One is left to wonder whether a female leader of Egypt would have been as harsh as this pharaoh is presented as being. Had the government of Egypt been dominated by women would they have been so abusive of the Hebrew people?
- What might the author of Exodus be trying to tell us by naming the midwives – Shiphrah and Puah – but not the pharaoh?
- Why do you think the author uses the Hebrew word *tevah*, which means "ark," instead of the Hebrew word for basket? Given that those who hear the story in Hebrew undoubtedly make the mental link to the story of Noah, do you find it odd that English translations render the word "basket"? Why or why not?
- Reflect on each woman in the story. How did they break the law? How were they honoured or rewarded for that?
- Who are the women you know – from history, or from your own life and community – who have acted in ways similar to one or more of the women in this story? What were the results?
- The book of Exodus could simply have begun with something like, "The Hebrews were kept as slaves by the Egyptians and God sent someone named Moses to lead them to freedom." Instead, we are given this story of several courageous women who conspire to bring about God's plans. Why might that be?
- The rabbis suggested that the princess had some kind of skin disease that would have made her an outcast. What does this insight add to the story? What has been your experience of different groups of "outcasts" working together?
- What are we invited to take from this story?
- Why do you think Miriam is called a prophet in Exodus 15:20? What makes her act of leading the women in a dance prophetic?

- To which other biblical woman would you give the title "prophet"?

- If we remember that the Hebrew people fled Egypt in a hurry – such a hurry, in fact, that they did not have time to let their bread rise – it might seem odd that the women took along musical instruments. What inspired them to do this, do you think?

SESSION 7

Two Fiery Women: Deborah and Jael

The story of Deborah, judge and prophet, is told twice in the Bible, in Judges 4 and Judges 5. The former is prose, and the latter is poetry. Judges 5 is much older – indeed, it is often considered one of the oldest pieces in the entire Bible.[13] Specifically, it is thought that Judges 5 may be the only portion of that book from the actual time of the Judges, which was the 11th and 12th century BCE. Accordingly, we will look at Judges 5 first, and then at Judges 4.

However, one significant piece from Judges 4 is worth mentioning at the outset, and that comes in verse 4: "Deborah, a prophet, the wife of Lappidoth [or "a fiery woman"] was a leader of Israel at that time." What is of significance here is that this is stated so matter-of-factly. No fuss is made of the fact that a woman served as judge, which meant ruler at that time. The vast majority of judges were male, according to the Bible, so the fact that a woman is named without any mention that she is unique, or that she is an oddity, is quite remarkable. The text suggests that Deborah stands equal to all the other judges, regardless of gender.

Similarly, we are used to women being named as "wife of ..." or "daughter of ..." because a woman's identity came through the man to whom she was attached. Deborah could be named as "wife of Lappidoth," which is where English-language translations default, but many add a footnote to say that just as legitimate to translate the Hebrew text as "wife of torches," which was not an uncommon way of describing someone as "fiery." Given the brief portion of her story that we are presented with it is quite probable that "fiery" is what was implied here. To be clear, "fiery" is not a gender-specific term; either a man or a woman could be fiery. These few words in Judges 4:4 present Deborah in a highly favourable and unbiased way – she is simply another in the line of judges of

Israel. Later in chapters 4 and 5 we will learn she had other traits as well.

Robert G. Boling[14] points out that there were many female prophets in ancient times; the word was not as confined to males as we might at first think, given the way the Bible has been presented to us through the ages.

Finally, it's worth noting that the story of Deborah influenced the work of George Frideric Handel, who composed an oratorio based on her story, which was hugely popular in its day.

Judges 5

At that time, Deborah and Barak, Abinoam's son, sang:
²When hair is long in Israel,
    when people willingly offer themselves – bless the Lord!
³Hear, kings!
    Listen, rulers!
I, to the Lord,
    I will sing.
I will make music to the Lord,
    Israel's God.
⁴Lord, when you set out from Seir,
    when you marched out from Edom's fields, the land shook,
    the sky poured down,
    the clouds poured down water.
⁵The mountains quaked
    before the Lord, the one from Sinai,
    before the Lord, the God of Israel.
⁶In the days of Shamgar, Anath's son,
    in the days of Jael, caravans ceased.
Those traveling by road
    kept to the backroads.
⁷Villagers disappeared;
    they disappeared in Israel,
        until you, Deborah, arose,
        until you arose as a mother in Israel.
⁸When they chose new gods,
    then war came to the city gates.
Yet there wasn't a shield or spear to be seen
    among forty thousand in Israel!

> [BIBLE STUDY]
> HEBREW SCRIPTURES
> **Women in the Bible**
> FOR Progressive Christians

⁹*My heart is with Israel's commanders,*
  who willingly offered themselves among the people –
    bless the Lord!
¹⁰*You who ride white donkeys,*
  who sit on saddle blankets,
  who walk along the road: tell of it.
¹¹*To the sound of instruments at the watering places,*
  there they repeat the Lord's victories,
    his villagers' victories in Israel.
Then the Lord's people marched down to the city gates.
¹²*"Wake up, wake up, Deborah!*
  Wake up, wake up, sing a song!
Arise, Barak!
  Capture your prisoners,
    Abinoam's son!"
¹³*Then those who remained marched down against royalty;*
  the Lord's people marched down against warriors.
¹⁴*From Ephraim they set out into the valley,*
  after you, Benjamin, with your people!
From Machir commanders marched down,
  and from Zebulun those carrying the official's staff.
¹⁵*The leaders of Issachar came along with Deborah;*
  Issachar was attached to Barak,
  and was sent into the valley behind him.
Among the clans of Reuben
  there was deep soul-searching.
¹⁶*"Why did you stay back among the sheep pens,*
  listening to the music for the flocks?"
For the clans of Reuben
  there was deep soul-searching.
¹⁷*Gilead stayed on the other side of the Jordan,*
  and Dan, why did he remain with the ships?
Asher stayed by the seacoast,
  camping at his harbours.
¹⁸*Zebulun is a people that readily risked death;*
  Naphtali too in the high countryside.
¹⁹*Kings came and made war;*
  the kings of Canaan fought
    at Taanach by Megiddo's waters,
      but they captured no spoils of silver.
²⁰*The stars fought from the sky;*

> from their orbits they fought against Sisera.
> ²¹The Kishon River swept them away;
>   the advancing river, the Kishon River.
>   March on, my life, with might!
> ²²Then the horses' hooves pounded
>   with the galloping, galloping of their stallions.
> ²³"Curse Meroz," says the Lord's messenger,
>   "curse its inhabitants bitterly,
>   because they didn't come to the Lord's aid,
>   to the Lord's aid against the warriors."
> ²⁴May Jael be blessed above all women;
>   may the wife of Heber the Kenite
>   be blessed above all tent-dwelling women.
> ²⁵He asked for water, and she provided milk;
>   she presented him cream in a majestic bowl.
> ²⁶She reached out her hand for the stake,
>   her strong hand for the worker's hammer.
> She struck Sisera;
>   she crushed his head;
>   she shattered and pierced his skull.
> ²⁷At her feet he sank, fell, and lay flat;
>   at her feet he sank, he fell;
>   where he sank, there he fell – dead.
> ²⁸Through the window she watched,
>   Sisera's mother looked longingly through the lattice.
> "Why is his chariot taking so long to come?
>   Why are the hoofbeats of his chariot horses delayed?"
> ²⁹Her wisest attendants answer;
>   indeed, she replies to herself:
> ³⁰"Wouldn't they be finding and dividing the loot?
>   A girl or two for each warrior;
>   loot of colored cloths for Sisera;
>   loot of colored, embroidered cloths;
>   two colored, embroidered cloths
>   as loot for every neck."
> ³¹May all your enemies perish like this, Lord!
>   But may your allies be like the sun, rising in its strength.
> And the land was peaceful for forty years.

The last verse first, which says the land was peaceful for 40 years, suggests that this was also the length of Deborah's term as a judge, although we cannot be sure. That she was a judge for such a lengthy time suggests that she was both young and extremely popular – either for the people to have wanted her as leader for that extended period of time, or, in the biblical way of thinking, for God to have blessed her with such a long life. This says a great deal about Deborah.

Judges 5 is generally known as the "song of Deborah" and was, as the first verse tells us, sung by Deborah and Barak. Some have suggested that it was written by a woman, which makes it stand out from the majority of biblical texts, which were written by men.

The song is placed at a time when "hair is long in Israel," literally. This is a euphemism for people offering themselves, or participating, willingly; a preferred translation might be something like "when they cast off restraint in Israel."[15] In other words, things are good – the time of Deborah's rule is a period when people are content and willing to support the government – in this case, the judge – without hesitation. We are told in verse 7 that Deborah was seen as mother of the nation, and that the people's willingness to serve stemmed from this fact.

Towards the end of the song, we encounter a significant story from Judges 4, told here in a rather different form. This is the story of Jael, a woman remembered for a single, violent act. Sisera, the leader of the enemy with whom Israel is at war, runs to Jael's tent. Interestingly, this is in the opposite direction of his troops, suggesting he is running away. The story in this account is told simply and bluntly; he asked for water and she provided milk, then reached out for a stake and drove it through his skull. He fell down dead at her feet.

The attention then shifts to Sisera's mother, gazing out her window, waiting for him to return. She and her attendants answer her wondering by assuming that Sisera and his army must have won the battle and are spending their time dividing the booty – booty that includes lots of beautiful fabric, and women who, presumably, will be kept as slaves. Something frequently overlooked but present in the text, then, is the fact that Jael didn't just kill an enemy but prevented him from taking the local woman hostage as sex slaves.

Some have seen here a link between the women of Israel and the "comfort women" of Korea and other countries who were enslaved by the Imperial Japanese Army. Estimates of the number of women taken vary greatly – the official Japanese record suggests 20,000 while Chinese records suggest a number closer to 500,000. The army sought to defend its actions by claiming these women served only as sexual outlets for their soldiers, claiming this would minimize war-time rape. Others, of course, see this as a slim and vain attempt to justify a horrific atrocity. In 2007, the Japanese government finally acknowledged the comfort women and issued an apology. Some ancient commentators used the fact that Jael prevented a similar situation as a justification of her actions.

Now let's turn to the story as it was retold in Judges 4 at a much later date – probably around 550 BCE. This version provides more details about the battle between Israel and the army of Sisera.

Judges 4

After Ehud had died, the Israelites again did things that the Lord saw as evil. ²So the Lord gave them over to King Jabin of Canaan, who reigned in Hazor. The commander of his army was Sisera, and he was stationed in Harosheth-ha-goiim. ³The Israelites cried out to the Lord because Sisera had nine hundred iron chariots and had oppressed the Israelites cruelly for twenty years.

⁴Now Deborah, a prophet, the wife of Lappidoth, was a leader of Israel at that time. ⁵She would sit under Deborah's palm tree between Ramah and Bethel in the Ephraim highlands, and the Israelites would come to her to settle disputes. ⁶She sent word to Barak, Abinoam's son, from Kedesh in Naphtali and said to him, "Hasn't the Lord, Israel's God, issued you a command? 'Go and assemble at Mount Tabor, taking ten thousand men from the people of Naphtali and Zebulun with you. ⁷I'll lure Sisera, the commander of Jabin's army, to assemble with his chariots and troops against you at the Kishon River, and then I'll help you overpower him.'"

⁸Barak replied to her, "If you'll go with me, I'll go; but if not, I won't go."

⁹Deborah answered, "I'll definitely go with you. However, the path you're taking won't bring honor to you, because the Lord will hand over Sisera to a woman." Then Deborah got up and went with Barak to Kedesh. ¹⁰He summoned Zebulun and Naphtali to Kedesh, and ten thousand men marched out behind him. Deborah marched out with him too.

¹¹Now Heber the Kenite had moved away from the other Kenites, the descendants of Hobab, Moses' father-in-law, and had settled as far away as Elon-bezaanannim, which is near Kedesh.

¹²When it was reported to Sisera that Barak, Abinoam's son, had marched up to Mount Tabor, ¹³Sisera summoned all of his nine hundred iron chariots and all of the soldiers who were with him from Harosheth-ha-goiim to the Kishon River. ¹⁴Then Deborah said to Barak, "Get up! This is the day that the Lord has handed Sisera over to you. Hasn't the Lord gone out before you?" So Barak went down from Mount Tabor with ten thousand men behind him. ¹⁵The Lord threw Sisera and all the chariots and army into a panic before Barak; Sisera himself got down from his chariot and fled on foot. ¹⁶Barak pursued the chariots and the army all the way back to Harosheth-ha-goiim, killing Sisera's entire army with the sword. No one survived.

¹⁷Meanwhile, Sisera had fled on foot to the tent of Jael, the wife of Heber the Kenite, because there was peace between Hazor's King Jabin and the family of Heber the Kenite. ¹⁸Jael went out to meet Sisera and said to him, "Come in, sir, come in here. Don't be afraid." So he went with her into the tent, and she hid him under a blanket.

¹⁹Sisera said to her, "Please give me a little water to drink. I'm thirsty." So she opened a jug of milk, gave him a drink, and hid him again. ²⁰Then he said to her, "Stand at the entrance to the tent. That way, if someone comes and asks you, 'Is there a man here?' you can say, 'No.'"

²¹But Jael, Heber's wife, picked up a tent stake and a hammer. While Sisera was sound asleep from exhaustion, she tiptoed to him. She drove the stake through his head and down into the ground, and he died. ²²Just then, Barak arrived after chasing Sisera. Jael went out to meet him and said, "Come and

BIBLE STUDY

HEBREW
SCRIPTURES
**Women in
the Bible**
FOR
Progressive
Christians

HEBREW SCRIPTURES
Women in the Bible
FOR Progressive Christians

I'll show you the man you're after." So he went in with her, and there was Sisera, lying dead, with the stake through his head.

²³So on that day God brought down Canaan's King Jabin before the Israelites. ²⁴And the power of the Israelites grew greater and greater over Canaan's King Jabin until they defeated him completely.

Clearly Deborah is a commanding figure, as Barak, a leader of the Israelite army, does not want to go into battle without her. She teases him, pointing out that she's willing to go but people will note that she and not Barak won the victory. Together they lead 10,000 soldiers into battle.

Sisera runs away, fleeing to the tent of Jael. She sneakily invites him in and hides him under a blanket. When he falls asleep, she kills him with the hammer and tent peg, then proudly shows her work to Barak.

Female violence

Sometimes when people first encounter Jael's story, they are appalled by her act of extreme violence. To be sure, Jael's actions are shocking, but do we respond with revulsion because of the act itself, or because Jael is a woman, or both? Female violence does not fit common notions or stereotypes of culturally appropriate "female behaviour," and acts of extreme violence even less so. Do we sometimes judge the violence of women more harshly because of this? While there is some evidence that courts tend to be more lenient with women, others dispute this finding, and in any event the court of public opinion is a different matter.

To be clear, today we hope and strive to avoid *all* acts of violence. At the same time, it's good to be aware of how our judgments against specific acts of violence may be biased based on gender. To offer an extreme example, would we judge a woman who kills her child differently (perhaps more harshly) than we would judge a father who commits the same act? Are the actions of one more incomprehensible than the actions of the other?

One thing can be said for sure. While both males and females are entirely capable of violence, even extreme violence, there are clear gender differences. Especially in domestic cases, female physical violence is typically an act of self-defence whereas for men it is typically an act of aggression, or an assertion of "power over"; also, females typically suffer far greater injuries.

We know virtually nothing about Jael; she appears nowhere else in the Bible. Her role, while significant in this particular moment, appears small overall. Yet we should be curious about the fact that the ancient rabbis noted that God chose Queen Esther for a particular moment in history, and that God chose others in a similar fashion – including Deborah and Jael. It seems that in the heat of these moments, it took a woman to get the job done.

Significantly, this is the last battle Israel fought for 40 years. Is this because it was so decisive? Is it because the defeated enemy was humiliated even more than normal because their defeat came at the hands of a woman? Is it because of Jael's violent act? We can't know. But clearly this is a vital story, and a vital moment.

Deborah is known as fiery, as a judge, as a prophet, and as the mother of the nation. Powerful stuff.

Questions

■ Why might the story of Deborah have been told?
■ How are Deborah and Jael similar to – or different from – other biblical women?
■ Reflect on the rather casual way the author of Judges 4 mentions that Deborah was a judge and prophet. What might this say about the leadership roles of women at this particular time?
■ Why do you think we have two versions of Deborah's story? Specifically, why might chapter 4 have been written? How does it change the perspective of the story?
■ What is your emotional reaction to Jael's act? Would your reaction have been different if it was a male who had committed this act?

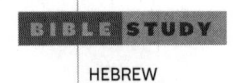

- How does the fact that Jael's actions likely prevented hundreds of women from being taken as sex slaves change your thoughts about her story?
- Deborah's time as a judge appears to have been both lengthy and peaceful, yet we are not told any of the details beyond this story. Do some imagining about how her time as judge might have been.
- As this study concludes, how has your understanding of the role of biblical women changed?
- What do you take from this study that might change the way you read and interact with scripture in the future?

Endnotes

1. Peter A. Pitzele, *Scripture Windows: Toward a Practice of Bibliodrama* (San Francisco: Alef Designs, 1997), 84.
2. Irvin A. Busenitz, "Woman's Desire for Man: Genesis 3:16 Reconsidered," in *Grace Theological Journal* 7.2 (1986), 203–12.
3. Carol M. Bechtel, *Esther: Interpretation: a Bible Commentary for Teaching and Preaching* (Louisville: John Knox, 2002), 16.
4. https://www.bibleodyssey.org/en/people/related-articles/levirate-marriage
5. David Bale, "The God with Breasts: El Shaddai in the Bible," from *History of Religions*, February 1982, Vol. 21, No. 3, pp. 240–256. Published by University of Chicago Press.
6. Accessed February 6, 2021, from https://en.wikipedia.org/wiki/Sarah
7. Rabbi Adam Morris, "Why Do Biblical Names Change," *Seasons of the Spirit,* https://www.seasonsonline.ca/11/81/news/page/2
8. See https://reformjudaism.org/exodus-not-fiction
9. See https://www.pbs.org/wgbh/nova/bible/meyers.html
10. *Exodus Rabbah* 1.14
11. Michael E. Williams, ed., *The Storyteller's Companion to the Bible: Volume 2: Exodus – Joshua* (Nashville: Abingdon, 1992), 24.
12. *Exodus Rabbah*, 1.23.
13. Williams, *The Storyteller's Companion to the Bible: Volume 4: Old Testament Women* (Nashville: Abingdon, 1993), 85.
14. Robert G. Boling, *Judges: A New Translation with Introduction and Commentary* (New York: Doubleday, 1975), 95.
15. Ibid., 107.

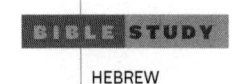

Bibliography

David Bale, "The God with Breasts: El Shaddai in the Bible," *History of Religions* 21, no. 3 (1982): 240–256.

Bechtel, Carol M. *Esther: Interpretation: A Bible Commentary for Teaching and Preaching.* Louisville: John Knox, 2002.

Boling, Robert G. *Judges: A New Translation with Introduction and Commentary.* New York: Doubleday, 1975.

Brueggemann, Walter. *Genesis: Interpretation: a Bible Commentary for Teaching and Preaching.* Louisville: John Knox Press, 1982.

Busenitz, Irvin A. "Woman's Desire for Man: Genesis 3:16 Reconsidered." *Grace Theological Journal* 7.2 (1986): 203–12.

Campbell, Edward F. Jr. *Ruth: A New Translation with Introduction and Commentary.* New York: Doubleday, 1975.

Fox, Michael V. *Character and Ideology in the Book of Esther.* Grand Rapids: Eerdmanns, 2001.

Levine, Amy-Jill. "Ruth." In *The Women's Bible Commentary*, edited by Carol A. Newsom and Sharon H. Ringe, 78–84. Louisville: Westminster John Knox Press, 1992.

Morris, Rabbi Adam. "Why Do Biblical Names Change." *Seasons of the Spirit.* https://www.seasonsonline.ca/11/81/news/page/2

Pitzele, Peter A. *Scripture Windows: Toward a Practice of Bibliodrama.* San Francisco: Alef Designs, 1997.

Trible, Phyllis. *God and the Rhetoric of Sexuality.* Minneapolis: Augsburg Fortress, 1986.

Williams, Michael E., ed. *The Storyteller's Companion to the Bible: Volume 2: Exodus – Joshua.* Nashville: Abingdon, 1992.

— *The Storyteller's Companion to the Bible: Volume 4, Old Testament Women.* Nashville: Abingdon, 1993.

ALSO AVAILABLE FROM WOOD LAKE

BIBLE STUDIES SERIES
for Progressive Christians

Marcus Borg once said we should take the Bible seriously, but not literally. Wood Lake Publishing's series of study guides ... *for Progressive Christians* seeks to do just that.

Author Donald Schmidt has a passionate love for the stories of the Bible, stories that have shaped individual Christians and the church for centuries. But sometimes the stories get buried by tradition, and sometimes they get misused and mistreated. This series of studies digs behind the layers of tradition and instead opens the scriptures in a way that invites us to determine our own understanding. What can faith stories written millennia ago tell us about how to live today? How is God's call for justice relevant in an age of computers, global warming, and pandemics? How can we find simple truths in these ancient texts?

These guides are perfect for individual and group use. Take time by yourself or join with others in a formal or informal study and you will find yourself immersed in wondrous story, freed from any sense that "this is what you must believe" and able to form or develop your own interpretation of texts that are still relevant and vital for today's living.

Each book is 5.5" x 8" | 80–100 pp | paperback | $14.95

To learn more about Donald Schmidt's work and to join Bible studies he offers on his books from time to time, go to:
www.revdonald.ca

WOOD LAKE
Imagining, living, and telling the faith story.

WOOD LAKE IS THE FAITH STORY COMPANY.

It has told
- the story of the seasons of the earth, the people of God, and the place and purpose of faith in the world;
- the story of the faith journey, from birth to death;
- the story of Jesus and the churches that carry his message.

Wood Lake has been telling stories for more than 35 years. During that time, it has given form and substance to the words, songs, pictures, and ideas of hundreds of storytellers.

Those stories have taken a multitude of forms – parables, poems, drawings, prayers, epiphanies, songs, books, paintings, hymns, curricula – all driven by a common mission of serving those on the faith journey.

Wood Lake Publishing Inc.

485 Beaver Lake Road
Kelowna, BC, Canada V4V 1S5
250.766.2778

www.woodlake.com